For Mike & Aldla,
Always make more time to
savor the Kansas Outdoors!

Michael Pearce
3-31-2015

Michael Pearce's
TASTE OF
the
KANSAS OUTDOORS
Cookbook

MICHAEL PEARCE'S
TASTE OF THE KANSAS OUTDOORS COOKBOOK

BY MICHAEL PEARCE

A PUBLICATION OF THE WICHITA EAGLE AND BEACON PUBLISHING CO. INC.

Original material by Michael Pearce published in The Wichita Eagle
© 2007, 2008, 2012, 2013, 2014 by The Wichita Eagle, Wichita, Kansas

Cover credits:
Photography by Bo Rader/The Wichita Eagle

Front cover inset photo by Michael Pearce/The Wichita Eagle

Design by Lyndsey Stafford/Armstrong Chamberlin

Photo credits:
Michael Pearce/The Wichita Eagle, pages 6-7, 8, inset 10-11, 12, 15, 19 top, 20, 24, 28, 32, 36, 40, 44, 48, 52, 56, 58-59, inset 60-61,
62, 65, 68, 72, 76, 84, 86-87, inset 88-89, 90, 93, 94, 95, 98, 100, 102, 104, 108, 110, 112, 114-115, inset 116-117, 121, 122-123, 130-131,
inset 132-133, 134, 137, 142, 146-147, 152, 156, 158-159, inset 160-161, left and center 166-167, inset top and middle 170-171, 174-175,
177; Bo Rader,/The Wichita Eagle, 10-11, 16, 18, center 19, 22, 26, 30, 34, 38, 42, 46, 50, 54, 60-61, 66-67, 70, 74, 78, 82, 88-89, 96, 106,
116-117, 118, 124, 128, 132-133, 138-139, 140, 144, 148, 150, 154, 160-161, 162, 165, 167, 168, 170-171, inset bottom, 170-171, 172-173,
178; Travis Heying/The Wichita Eagle, 19, 80, 126.

Book design: Lyndsey Stafford/Armstrong Chamberlin

MICHAEL PEARCE'S TASTE OF THE KANSAS OUTDOORS COOKBOOK © 2014 by The Wichita Eagle and Beacon Publishing Co. Inc.
www.kansas.com/outdoors

Printed 2014 by Mennonite Press Inc., Newton, Kansas

ISBN 978-0-692-28850-4

Library of Congress Control Number: 2014950589

TABLE OF CONTENTS

Smoky Hills sunrise   Wilson Reservoir

Checking in – Edwards County

INTRODUCTION

According to family members, my interest in the outdoors precedes my earliest memories. Faded black-and-white photos show me toting a fish that looks almost as long as I was, or following my father afield as I toted a toy shotgun held perfectly at port arms.

The outdoors lifestyle is the only one I've ever known or wanted. It's what I've done in my free time and as my profession, and includes the food I've eaten.

Wild fish and game have been our main meals since my wife, Kathy, and I married in 1980. The economics of not having to buy meat was a major force back when we treated dollars like diamonds.

Even when careers brought more money, we stuck with things like venison and pheasant rather than beef and chicken. They've always been a welcome byproduct of my occupation as an outdoors writer. A deep respect for all the fish and game I've gotten has pushed me to make the most of every ounce of such meat.

Though she doesn't hunt, Kathy has come to feel the same dedication. Our daughter, Lindsey, and son, Jerrod, were brought up with similar respect for the animal and the process. Both have earned their share of fish and game, from pre-hunt preparation and making a humane shot to processing the meat and not wasting a bite at the table. As they matured, their research into healthy diets helped strengthen their dedication to wild game.

But one of the main reasons we've eaten so many tons of everything from tiny bluegill to huge moose is because it can be as delicious as it is healthy. On the rare times we eat out, we seldom leave a restaurant thinking we've had a better meal than things we make at home.

Through the years we've cooked and served our favorites to hundreds of people, including those at our popular Beast Feast wild-game dinners. Our dinners generally include 8 to 10 courses. Many who arrived swearing that everything we served would be "gamey" and tough raved as they came back for seconds or thirds and, eventually, asked for the recipes.

I've always been glad to share the recipes then, and I'm glad to share them now.

Michael Pearce

► If you're looking for fancy, complex recipes, look elsewhere. I've lived by the motto that a meal shouldn't take longer to prepare than consume. (Long cooking and marinating times excluded.)

► I figure 70 percent of our success goes back to how the meat is treated from the time it's shot or landed until it hits the heat of cooking. Please pay attention to sections on meat care and trimming.

► These recipes are more guidelines than exact formulas. They are meant to be tweaked, adjusted, substituted and rearranged. In the recipes you'll probably notice I have a fondness of fresh lime juice, liquid smoke, minced garlic and cilantro, but am a bit of a wuss when it comes to chili peppers. If you don't like garlic, leave it out. If you eat habaneros like I do cashews, throw some in.

► Adapt to what you have on hand. When our garden is in full swing, I'll hand-squeeze tomatoes only minutes from the vine into about anything.

► Saved time is good time. Commercial marinades are always faster, and often cheaper, than what you can make from scratch. When my recipes call for minced garlic, I use pre-minced from a jar.

► A sharp trimming knife is a must. Remember a $10 fish fillet knife, that regularly sees a $10 sharpener, is superior to a $200 knife that's dull.

► Cooking times could vary from what the recipe recommends, especially with variations in the sizes of cuts and temperatures of grills. A fast digital meat thermometer can be purchased for less than $30, removing much of the guesswork from cooking.

► Grilling will be much easier if you "season" the grate regularly by rubbing it with grapeseed oil. Such a coating will help prevent any meat, especially fish, from sticking during the cooking process.

► The main thing that will serve you well is a positive attitude and confidence that as food, wild game and fish can not only be good, it can be great,. Believe you can follow these meat care tips and recipes in this cookbook toward positive results. I promise, the better those wild meals taste, the more satisfaction you'll feel during your times afield and at the water for years to come.

BIG GAME

In his iconic journal on pre-civilization Kansas, J. R. Mead wrote glowingly of vast buffalo herds from the Flint Hills westward.

Through his eyes, we read of cresting a Smoky Hill's ridge, possibly in what's now Russell County, and seeing not only buffalo, but herds of elk and deer and pronghorn antelope.

It's no wonder he named the valley's stream Paradise Creek.

Kansas has changed much since Mead's long-ago visit and descriptions. Farms, ranches, towns and roads have eaten away much of what was unbroken prairie. But Kansas is still like a paradise for those who pursue big game.

We have enough whitetail deer to warrant more than four months of open seasons. No matter the month, Kansas whitetails are masters at survival, and are often only seen heading over the next rise, namesake bright tail wagging from side-to-side like a wave goodbye.

Our mule deer are creatures of the western one-third of the state, living well in broken canyons and seemingly endless seas of prairie grass. A mature mule deer buck looks as thick as a boxcar, yet covers ground like a race car with its famed pogo-like bounce.

But even that is slow compared to the pronghorns, North America's fastest mammal, that live in the wide-open spaces of far western Kansas, where their binocular-like eyes can spot an approaching hunter a mile or more away. And pronghorns aren't shy about showing off that speed. Sometimes a herd will streak off just because it can, and like a flock of blackbirds follow one directly behind the other in crack-the-whip style.

Our buffalo are confined to fenced lands. Free-ranging elk, it appears, are reclaiming some of their original range. There's a sizable herd on Fort Riley, and building numbers along any river or drainage that comes from the west.

Dining daily on lush prairies and bountiful cropfields make Kansas big game some of the largest of their kind in the nation. Prepared properly, they're also some of the most flavorful, too.

Nicholas Santonastasso – Pawnee County

This is a story how a tiny Kansas town has rallied, every fall since 2001, to help kids with life-threatening illnesses enjoy a great deer hunt. It's yet another example of the deep kindness often found in rural Kansas. This story was originally published on Dec. 12, 2010.

The Wichita Eagle

SERIOUSLY ILL BOY GETS HUNT OF A LIFETIME IN LARNED

LARNED – With two heart transplants and ongoing coronary artery problems, 11-year-old Matthew Billy has spent most of his life watching other kids play baseball. Friday, the boy from Wister, Okla., hit the hunting world's version of a grand slam when he shot a magnificent 12-point buck.

He got his chance thanks to a small Kansas town with a huge heart.

Matthew and Nicholas Santonastasso were the guests at Larned's 10th annual Life Hunt, a deer hunt for children with life-threatening illnesses.

The hunt offers guided trips with all expenses paid - and ample small-town hospitality.

"I can't even call it a dream hunt because it's so far past anything we ever dreamed about for Nicholas," Michael Santonastasso said about his son. "It's a thrill just to know there are people out there that care. All they ask is to see the excitement on that child's face."

Nicholas, a 14-year-old from Bayville, N.J., was born without legs and has one finger on his only arm. Friday morning, he shot a heavy-horned nine-point buck with a thick body.

With a huge smile the boy repeatedly said,"He's so big, he's so big," as he touched the antlers.

His father watched with moistened eyes. Their guide, Tim Schaller, watched with a smile of satisfaction.

At his rural Larned home, Schaller has walls covered with big antlers. About 10 years ago he realized there was a better use for such a resource.

With several hunting buddies, he began Larned's Life Hunt.

They've had about two kids a year from about 10 states, most with progressive cancer or serious organ ailments.

To find children for the annual hunts, the Larned group works with national organizations that create opportunities for kids with life-threatening illnesses.

"We do what it takes. We've carried kids into stands and worked around their problems," Schaller said. "We can make it happen. It's worth every minute to see that smile when they get one."

Examples of specialization Life Hunt provides include customized shooting benches and special gun rests within roomy, well-hidden blinds.

With such a setup, Nicholas was able to aim the rifle with shoulder and chin movements until he squeezed the trigger with his finger.

The hunts are on about 2,000 leased acres of rolling sandhills of tall grass and wild plum thickets. The area carries many high-quality deer.

On Friday, both boys and their fathers watched a parade of whitetails pause at food plots about 30 yards away.

"Any of these bucks would be good bucks where we come

continued...

from in Oklahoma," whispered Simon Billy, Matthew's dad, as he watched an array of four- to eight-pointers pass. The boys didn't shoot until they saw an amazing buck.

"These kids haven't been sitting at home dreaming about just shooting a deer. They've been dreaming about shooting a trophy," Schaller said. "A lot of people shoot deer, but few people in the country ever shoot bucks like these kids get."

Michael Santonastasso agreed that taking a big buck added to the experience for his son.

"This gives him the chance to have the best of something," he said. "We just don't have these in New Jersey, and people are going to want to see it, they're going to want to hear about it. When we go home Nick will be the man. He'll be the one showing something off and telling the stories." The hunt's volunteer base is about 75, and is growing annually.

"Once people find out it's for these kids, they can't do enough," said Gordon Schartz, who cooks at a hunt fundraiser. "If you see the looks on these kids' faces one time, it makes all the difference in the world."

Everything is covered: snacks, travel costs, $300 deer permits and taxidermy mounts of the bucks.

When they learned Matthew didn't have a rifle that's legal for Kansas deer, the hunt's organizers bought him a new Browning bolt-action with a scope.

There's a fund-raising banquet and auction the night before the hunt. Some of the purchased items are given to the boys.

Schaller said people sometimes walk into his engineering office and hand him checks for up to $500 for the hunt.

After Friday's hunt, Schaller, several guides and his New Jersey guests were celebrating at a crowded restaurant.

Several locals stopped to chat with the boy about his buck.

One reached across the table and placed something in Schaller's hand. It was two folded $50 bills.

"See that, $100 and I don't even know that guy," he said. "That happens all the time. Isn't that great?"

UPDATE: Matthew Billy received his third heart transplant a few weeks after he left Larned's Life Hunt, according to Schaller. Matthew and Nicholas still stay in contact with the friends they made while in Kansas.

Every year since their hunt, Schaller and crew have succeeded in getting two deserving hunters a trophy-class buck. One of the boys in 2012 got his buck in the final seconds of the final day of the season. "We had some divine intervention getting him that buck," Schaller said. "We've had that several times."

The boy died a few months later.

Looking for does – Gove County

1. Don't let gender or age dissuade you from trying to get the best meat possible from any Kansas big game. I've had mature male Kansas whitetail, mule deer, elk and pronghorns provide tender meat with great flavor.

2. The less stress that goes into an animal before it's taken, the better. Animals that run far and fast just before or just after a shot can be tougher and stronger tasting as things similar to adrenaline spread through the muscles.

3. The quicker the meat is cleaned and cooled the better. Field dressing can help greatly, as can quickly getting the animal to a cold storage facility if the temperature is more than 35-40 degrees.

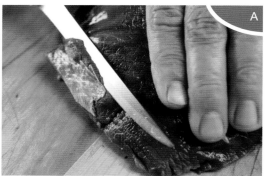

The flavor and tenderness of some roasts can be improved by removing the fat and membrane.

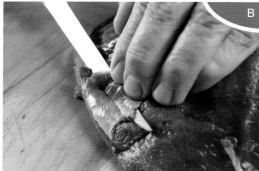

Remove the silvery membrane on the outside of roasts, and edges of some steaks, with a sharp knife.

The more membrane, the more toughness it will bring to the meat unless trimmed away.

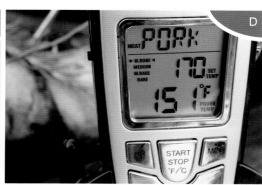

A digital meat thermometer makes exact cooking easier. Be sure wild pork is well-done.

4. Since I process my own game, I skin the animal in the field, removing the quarters, loins and neck meat, and get them on ice, or snow, in a cooler. It's easy, takes me about 30 minutes, and is legal as I use the state's online check-in system at www.ks.outdoors.com.

Using a system that does not remove the animal's entrails helps keep the meat clean, and in manageable pieces. (To learn how, go online and type "gutless method for cleaning deer" into a search engine.)

It also allows the hide, entrails and most of the bones to remain in nature, where other animals can benefit.

To keep the animal cool, put the cooler where it will be shaded all day and remove the stopper from one end while using a board or brick to raise the other end a few inches so melting ice drains. You can add ice, or jugs of frozen water, as needed.

5. If taking your big game to a commercial processor, insist they do not cut through any bone and that all external fat be removed before they cut into the meat.

Much of the "gamey" flavor associated with big game is within the marrow and fat. As much as fat and marbling add to the flavor of good beef, it detracts from good venison.

6. Don't be intimidated by the idea of processing your own big game. Again, a little looking online will show a wealth of ways to process anything from a small pronghorn to a giant bull elk with minimal time, effort and tools.

You can't mess it up. The muscles naturally separate where the meat should be cut into roasts. Any meat you cut away to shape up a roast can be used for stew meat or burger.

7. I normally process my big game 2 to 10 days after it's cooled. As with beef, aging the meat seems to help with the tenderness.

8. When it comes to actual preparation, remember that red meat is great meat, no matter the kind of big game. Use a thin, sharp knife and cut away any membrane on the outside of roasts or steaks, or away from anything you're wanting to grind for burger. It's worth the few extra minutes.

GRILLED VENISON LOIN

The meat from this amazingly simple recipe has been served as an appetizer to more than 1,000 people through the many years of Ed and Judy Markel's wild-game dinner in Pretty Prairie. So far, not one complaint.

One of the keys is that the loin, or backstrap as it's often called, is left in 8-inch to 10-inch sections, rather than cut into tiny steaks. The longer section of meat keeps it from drying so quickly on the grill, or being overpowered by the marinade.

The marinade, Zesty Italian Dressing, seems to have the perfect blend of seasonings and oils to compliment the venison's flavor and improve the tenderness. The thin bacon keeps the outside of the venison from drying out, but doesn't produce the flare-ups on the grill that thicker, fattier pork can produce.

WHAT YOU'LL NEED:

Prep time: 20 minutes, *plus extended marinating time*
Cooking time: 10-20 minutes
Difficulty: Requires some grilling skills

1 8-to-10-inch chunk of venison loin

1 small bottle Zesty Italian Dressing
(fat-free will work, if needed)

3-4 slices of low-sodium bacon

toothpicks
soaked in water 1 hour

Clean off the venison loin, trimming any fat or membrane. Place in a gallon sealable bag and pour in the Zesty Italian Dressing. Squeeze out the air and seal tightly.

Refrigerate 4-24 hours. I like the latter.

Preheat grill to medium-high (350-400 degrees).

Remove the meat from the marinade, hold over the sink to drip for a few seconds. On a flat surface, spiral wrap each piece of bacon around the loin so all the meat is covered. Fasten with toothpicks.

Place on the grill. The thin bacon shouldn't provide many flare-ups, but watch and be ready to move the meat to another part of the grill. Turn about every five minutes.

Cook until the internal temperature is medium-rare (130 degrees). Remove and let sit on a cutting board for about five minutes, so the meat absorbs any juices.

Remove the toothpicks and slice ¼-inch thick.

SAUTEED VENISON TENDERLOIN MEDALLIONS

The tenderloins of a deer are the filet mignon of venison. They're usually no longer than 10 inches and 1 inch in diameter, and sit just below the deer's spine. They're easily removed after the animal is field-dressed with a few strokes of a pocket knife.

I like to remove them as quickly as possible and get them into a plastic bag so they don't dry out.

A partial meal at best, the tenderloins should be fixed fresh and often the same evening the deer is killed. This is a super easy

WHAT YOU'LL NEED:

Prep time: 20 minutes
Cooking time: 20-30 minutes
Difficulty: Requires moderate grilling skills

venison tenderloins
cut into 1-inch sections

black pepper

salt

1 large onion
thinly sliced

½ tsp. minced garlic

4 tbs. butter

¾ cup sliced fresh mushrooms

4 tbs. flour *(optional)*

water *(optional)*

With the heel of your hand, flatten into ½-inch medallions. Sprinkle with salt and pepper. Melt 2 tbs. butter in a skillet on medium-high, saute the onions and garlic for a few minutes, then add the sliced mushrooms.

Remove when the vegetables are done, about 10 minutes. Add the rest of the butter and saute the venison 2 to 3 minutes per side.

If desired, add some flour to the drippings in the skillet and slowly stir in enough water to make a gravy. Serve with gravy poured over the meat and vegetables.

GROUND VENISON
ZUCCHINI BOATS

One of my favorite things about summer is walking into our garden and picking what we want to eat for dinner. This recipe is popular because of our great luck with growing zucchini, yellow squash and tomatoes.

I normally have a package of venison burger already thawed in the refrigerator so it's ready to go for a dozen or more recipes we like to use.

WHAT YOU'LL NEED:

Prep time: 30 minutes
Cooking time: 35-40 minutes
Difficulty: Easy

1 lb. venison burger

1 tsp. minced garlic

2 foot-long zucchinis

1 tomato
seeded and finely chopped

½ cup finely chopped mushrooms

½ tsp. dried basil

½ tsp. dried oregano

2 tbs. olive oil

½ cup Parmesan cheese

In a medium-high skillet, brown the venison burger with the minced garlic. Drain, and set aside. Preheat oven to 400 degrees.

Cut zucchini in half, lengthwise. Use a spoon to carefully scoop out the seeds and discard them. Carefully scoop the pulp from all four halves and finely chop the pulp.

Combine the pulp of the zucchinis, tomato, mushrooms, basil, oregano, olive oil and ¼ cup of cheese. Divide the browned venison evenly among the bottom of the four zucchini shells, then fill with the mixed ingredients.

Place the stuffed zucchini on a baking dish that's coated with cooking spray and cover "the boats" with foil. Bake for 25 minutes, or until the zucchini is tender. Sprinkle on the remaining cheese and bake, uncovered, another five minutes

NOTES:

► Any long squash, such as yellow summer squash, will also work.

CUSTOM-GRILLED VENISON BURGERS

Many years ago, our friend Kent Rains said his idea of gourmet cooking was sprinkling powdered Hidden Valley Ranch salad dressing on top of a package of hamburger, making it into patties and tossing them on the grill.

At the time we'd never heard of such a thing, but we've since gone through several pounds of powdered ranch dressing and had fun experimenting with other seasonings.

WHAT YOU'LL NEED:

Prep time: 10 minutes
Cooking time: 10-15 minutes
Difficulty: Requires some grilling skills

1-2 lbs. venison burger

1-4 oz. packet powdered
Hidden Valley Ranch salad dressing mix

1 ripe tomato

1 small onion

several leaves of romaine lettuce

hamburger buns

favorite condiments

Spread the venison burger across a plate or platter until it is about 1-inch thick. Carefully sprinkle powdered ranch dressing on the meat until there's a thin but even coating. Generally about half a packet per 1-1½ lbs. of meat.

Knead the burger until it is well-mixed, cover it and let sit in the refrigerator for ½ to 2 hours so the seasoning spreads.

Preheat the grill to 350-375 degrees, Grill four or five minutes per side, until medium-rare to medium, about 140 degrees.

Place the buns face down on the grill the last few minutes so they're lightly toasted.

NOTES:

► Onion can also be grilled by placing it in a small foil boat with a bit of butter.

► If the tomato isn't deep red and juicy, don't bother.

► Try other powdered spices and rubs. If needed, the burger can be divided before the spices are sprinkled on so everyone can have their favored flavor.

VENISON HAWAIIAN SLIDERS

The hardest part of this recipe can be finding the second-most important ingredient: pineapple preserves. Some grocery stores have it, but many do not. It can also be ordered online.

WHAT YOU'LL NEED:

Prep time: 30 minutes
Cooking time: 10-20 minutes
Difficulty: Requires some grilling skills

1¼ lb. venison burger

¼ cup + 2 tbs. pineapple preserves

½ cup mayonnaise

½ tsp. garlic powder

⅛ tsp. + ½ tsp. salt

¼ tsp. onion powder

¼ tsp. black pepper

6 slices pepper jack cheese
cut into quarters

1 12-count package of Hawaiian rolls
toasted

Combine mayonnaise, ¼ cup pineapple preserves and ⅛ tsp. salt in a small bowl and mix well. Refrigerate until needed.

In a larger bowl mix the venison burger with 2 tbs. pineapple preserves, garlic powder, ½ tsp. salt, black pepper and onion powder.

Preheat grill to medium-high about 350 degrees. Divide the meat mixture to make 12 equal-sized patties. Push a thumbprint into both sides to allow for swelling.

Grill to desired doneness. Remember, the small patties will cook very rapidly, so do not overcook and dry them out.

Place two squares of cheese on each patty after they've been turned for the final time. When done, place the patty on a toasted roll and top with the pineapple/mayonnaise mixture sauce.

NO HASSLE VENISON ROAST

One of the keys to cooking a good venison roast is cooking it long and low and not letting the meat get dry. Here's a simple way to make a good roast without a lot of work.

Roast cooked like this works great sliced thin for sandwiches. Or you can slice it thin, whip up some mashed potatoes and gravy and make some good ol' fashioned open-faced sandwiches.

8-pointer – Quivira National Wildlife Refuge

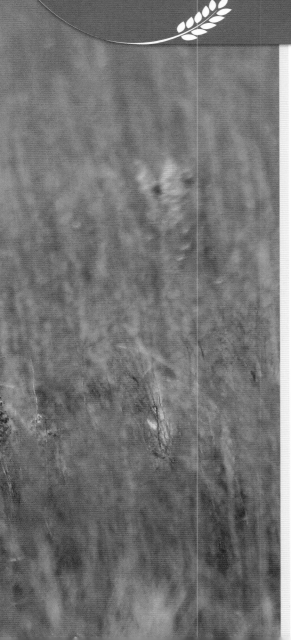

WHAT YOU'LL NEED:

Prep time: 30 minutes
Cooking time: 3 hours
Difficulty: Easy

2-3 lb. venison roast
fat and membrane trimmed away

1 oven roasting bag

2 large onions
sliced

4 tbs. butter

salt

pepper

garlic powder

1 package powdered onion soup mix

2 cups water

Pre-heat oven to 300 degrees. Rub all sides of the roast with the butter, sprinkle well with salt, pepper and garlic powder. Place roast and sliced onions in the roasting bag.

Dissolve the soup mix in the water and pour into the bag. Prepare the bag per instructions. Cook for about 3 hours, until the meat is tender. Remove roast from the bag, and cut into thin slices.

SMOKY HILLS 3 MEAT CHILI

The Smoky Hills of Kansas start north of Abilene and roll westward. It changes along the way from tallgrass prairie of towering bluestem grasses and vibrant flowers to short grass and spiny prickly pear and yucca further west.

It is a beautiful region with deep and jagged rock canyons, towering stone formations such as the Chalk Pyramids and an abundance of wildlife from tiny bobwhite quail to giant mule deer bucks with racks that look as wide as goal posts as they bounce away.

I named this chili in honor of the region because of the wild west flavor both hold. Yes, it makes a monster batch, but chili shouldn't be made any other way.

It freezes and shares well. A couple of gallons never lasts long in the newsroom at The Wichita Eagle on a cold, wintry day.

WHAT YOU'LL NEED:

Prep time: 30 minutes, *plus extended marinating time*
Cooking time: 1 hour
Difficulty: Easy

1½ lb. venison burger

2 lbs. venison roast, stew meat or round steak
diced into membrane-free 1-inch cubes

2 lbs. wild turkey or pheasant breast meat
diced into membrane-free 1-inch cubes

2 oz. package Williams Chili Seasoning
(4 lb. packet)

2 14.5 oz. cans diced tomatoes

1 15 oz. can black beans

1 15 oz. can pinto beans

1 15oz. can kidney beans

1 15 oz. can whole corn

1 small onion
diced

½ tsp. minced garlic

1 cup mesquite marinade

2 limes
juiced

⅓ bottle of liquid smoke

½ cup chopped cilantro

cooking oil

Place venison roast in sealable bag with mesquite marinade and let soak 1-2 hours.

Place turkey or pheasant in a sealable bag with lime juice, liquid smoke and cilantro and let soak 1-2 hours.

Heat 2 skillets to medium-high, about 350 degrees.

After marinating, drain and fry the venison and turkey or pheasant cubes separately until the meat is done. Use a small amount of cooking oil if needed. Place the meats into a large, deep cooking pot.

Brown hamburger with the diced small onion and garlic. Add it to the rest of the meat.

Add the rest of the ingredients, stirring well and let simmer for an hour or so, stirring often. Serves well with hand-crushed tortilla chips in the chili, carrot and celery sticks.

Gets its best flavor if stored 2 or 3 days before serving.

VENISON SALAD SANDWICHES

Leftover venison roast can be turned into super-easy sandwich spread that's moist, flavorful and fast to prepare.

For several years, I'd spend a late-summer day smoking all of the venison roasts we had left over from the previous seasons. I'd grind them all, place about three cups of the ground meat in sealable freezer bags and freeze. Placed in tepid water after work some afternoon, the ground meat thawed quickly and was ready for the other additives to make venison salad sandwiches.

This spread is usually mixed more on texture and taste than actual measurements, but these should get you close.

The stories it could tell – Gove County

WHAT YOU'LL NEED:

Prep time: 20 minutes
Cooking time: None needed
Difficulty: Easy with a grinder, not easy without

1 lb. cooked venison roast
ground or chopped extremely fine

¼ cup onion, minced

¼- to ½-cup sweet pickle relish

½ cup mayonnaise

½ cup barbecue sauce

¼ tsp. garlic powder

⅛ tsp. black pepper

¼ tsp. salt

Thoroughly mix all of the ingredients, and serve on bread.

EASIEST VENISON ROAST

With a family of busy people, this became one of the Pearce family favorites. It could be served anytime after 5 p.m. and was flat-out good.

Coming home from KU after her first semester, our daughter, Lindsey, asked for this to be made so she could walk into our house and be greeted by the smell of good food.

The venison will be fall-apart tender, thanks to being cooked long and low, with plenty of steam and flavor coming from the broth and veggies.

If the roast has some fat, thaw just enough to trim it away.

WHAT YOU'LL NEED:

Prep time: 15-20 minutes
Cooking time: 8-12 hours
Difficulty: Easy

1 frozen, de-boned venison roast of 2-4 lbs
exact cut not important

1 can condensed French onion soup

1 large potato

1 large onion

1 cup baby carrots

2 ribs of celery

seasoned salt

garlic pepper

Place the frozen roast in a slow cooker and season liberally. Cut the veggies into chunks and place around and on top of the meat.

Pour soup mixture on top, add a half-can of water and replace the lid. Cook on low 8 to 12 hours. When done, slice the meat thin, and save some of the juice in the slow cooker to pour over the slices.

NOTES:

► Works well with any big-game roast.

► A packet of instant gravy mix, with some of the juice from the roast, makes a great sauce to pour over the meat and vegetables.

PONY CREEK
VENISON MEATLOAF

Pony Creek cuts a serpentine path through southern Leavenworth County. It flows past our family farm, a location with the area's steepest bluffs, and hills covered in towering forests of five kinds of oaks, hickory and walnut. It has been our son, Jerrod's, private bowhunting ground since his college days.

As well as hundreds of hours of soul-soothing time outdoors, the farm has provided him with hundreds of meals. This is one of his favorite ways to use venison burger from deer that have been fattened on natural acorns, plots of clover, soybeans and corn.

Staredown – *Quivira National Wildlife Refuge*

WHAT YOU'LL NEED:

Prep time: 20 minutes
Cooking time: 45 minutes - 1 hour
Difficulty: Easy

1½-2 lbs. ground venison
(ground wild turkey or wild pig will also work)

1 medium onion
finely diced

1 egg, lightly beaten

1 tbs. Worcestershire sauce

1½ tsp. kosher salt

½ tsp. fresh ground black pepper

1 tbs. fresh thyme chopped
or 1 tsp. dried

1 tbs. fresh parsley chopped
or 1 tsp. dried

1 tbs. oregano chopped
or 1 tsp. dried

½ cup bread crumbs

⅓ cup ketchup *(optional)*

Preheat oven to 375 degrees. Mix all of the ingredients and form a loaf in a short-sided baking dish. Cover with ketchup if desired. Bake until the internal temperature is 160 degrees, or about 45 minutes to 1 hour, depending on the size and shape of the meatloaf. Remove, and let rest for 5 minutes before slicing.

VENISON MARINARA WITH VEGGIE NOODLES

During the garden months, my wife and I may eat zucchini or summer squash four nights a week in a variety of ways, including peeled in strips to replicate pasta.

Not only is it super healthy, it's quick and foolproof.

Sometimes I'll buy a tiny jar of prepared marinara sauce, then build it up with my own tomatoes, onion and garlic.

WHAT YOU'LL NEED:

Prep time: 30-45 minutes *if making sauce*
Cooking time: 1 1/2 - 2 hours
Difficulty: Easy

1 lb. venison burger

1 small onion
halved and finely diced separately

1 tsp. salt

1 tsp. white sugar

1 tsp. dried oregano

¼ tsp. black pepper

¼ tsp. garlic powder

3 cups ripe tomatoes
chopped fine

1 small can tomato paste

¾ cup sliced mushrooms

½ cup white wine *(optional)*

2-4 zucchini, summer squash or a combination

2 tbs. olive oil

½ tsp. minced garlic

Brown the venison burger with half of the chopped onion. Drain and remove. In a large pot, combine the remaining ingredients and stir. Bring to a simmer and add the meat. Let simmer 1-2 hours, or until desired thickness.

As the sauce is finishing, lay the squash on a flat surface and peel into ribbons using a potato peeler, julienne tool or mandolin. (If using a mandolin, be sure to wear a cut-proof kitchen glove. Don't ask me how I know this!)

In a skillet, heat olive oil to medium with the garlic and saute for a minute. Add the squash ribbons and saute briefly, no longer than 2 minutes. You want them vibrantly colored and still a bit crispy.

When sauce is thick enough, serve over a bed of squash ribbons.

VENISON PUMPKIN CHILI

I'll admit it, there's a little extra parental pride when you start getting some of your best recipes from your children. That's especially true in our family, where we've always had a family-based dedication to the outdoors and using every ounce of wild game we get. This recipe comes from my son, Jerrod.

WHAT YOU'LL NEED:

Prep time: 20 minutes
Cooking time: 30-45 minutes
Difficulty: Easy

2 lbs. ground venison or wild pork

1 large diced onion
divided in half

1½ tsp. minced garlic
divided in half

14 oz. can pumpkin puree
(not pie filling)

28 oz. roasted tomatoes
diced

15 oz. can tomato sauce

7 oz. can roasted green chilies
diced

1 cup chicken stock

olive oil

salt

pepper

CHILI SPICES

2 tbs. chili powder

2 tbs. cumin

1 tbs. paprika

2 tsp. salt

2 tsp. coriander

2 tsp. cinnamon

2 tsp. cocoa

1 tsp. garlic powder

¼ tsp. cayenne pepper

Mix together the chili spices, then add 1 tbs. olive oil to a large pot, heat to medium-high and brown the meat with half of the minced onion and half of the minced garlic. Add the pumpkin to the pan with the meat and stir until the pumpkin is heated. Add the rest of the ingredients, heating and stirring until well mixed.

BTE ELK BURGERS (BETTER THAN EVER)

I've had some pretty good runs of elk meat, including taking two huge bulls in one fall. Next to moose, it's my favorite meat. That's meant some great steaks, roasts and, blessedly, scores of dinners of elk burgers.

Well-handled elk, or moose, doesn't need much doctoring to be delicious. Still, sometimes it's fun to kick things up a bit.

WHAT YOU'LL NEED:

Prep time: 30 minutes
Cooking time: 10-15 minutes
Difficulty: Requires moderate grilling skills

2 lbs. ground elk

⅓ cup mayonnaise

1 tsp. Dijon mustard

1 tsp. horseradish

1 1/2 tsp. lime juice

½ tsp. zested lime

3 tbs. plain yogurt

½ cup finely chopped green onions

½ tsp. salt

½ tsp. black pepper

1 tsp. Worcestershire sauce

8 hamburger buns

3 tbs. melted butter

½ tsp. garlic powder

Pre-heat grill to 350 degrees. Combine mayonnaise, lime zest, lime juice, mustard and horseradish in a small bowl. Refrigerate until ready to use as a dip or spread.

In a larger bowl, combine salt, pepper, onions, Worcestershire sauce and yogurt. Crumble the elk meat over the mixture and mix well, then form into 8 patties.

Using your thumb, make a slight depression into both sides of each patty to compensate for swelling while cooking.

Brush the melted butter, combined with garlic, on the faces of the buns.

Cook burgers, turning occasionally, until medium-rare (130 degrees). While the meat is cooking, add the buns to the grill, flat side down until toasted and grill marks appear.

NOTES:

► A slice of cheese can be added to each patty after they're turned for the final time.

► Patties will also cook nicely on a George Foreman-style electric grill for a total of 3 minutes.

VENISON CABBAGE ROLLS AND SAUERKRAUT

I was 17 when I shot my first whitetail on our farm. As bad luck had it, it was about as old and I was clueless on all counts of meat preparation.

The old deer was processed incorrectly. We tried repeatedly to cook it like beef. We overcooked it, we cooked it bone-in and didn't trim any membrane or fat. I ate it because I was proud of it. But the first time I ever really appreciated it was when my stepmother, Nancy, made venison cabbage rolls from the buck.

Nancy is the person who taught me that there is always a way to make wild game great. Nearly 40 years after that first deer, we still trade wild-game recipes.

Early-morning buck – Pawnee County

WHAT YOU'LL NEED:

Prep time: 45 minutes

Cooking time: 1 1/2 hours

Difficulty: Easy, *but rolling the meat and rice in the cabbage leaves can be tedious.*

1-1 ½ lbs. of venison burger

1 lb. pork sausage
unseasoned

1 head of cabbage
core removed and leaves separated, stem area removed

¾ cup raw rice

½ minced onion

salt

pepper

1 large can sauerkraut

1 cup tomato juice

Boil leaves from the cabbage until they are pliable and can be rolled.

Mix the venison, pork, rice and onion, adding salt and pepper to taste.

Place a 1-inch layer of sauerkraut in the bottom of a Dutch oven or similar deep cooking pan with a lid.

Put enough of the meat mixture in the center of a leaf of cabbage for the leaf to roll back over itself top and bottom. Place roll on the layer of sauerkraut. Keep making rolls and stacking them side-by-side. When the layer is complete, add another layer of sauerkraut and repeat until you're out of cabbage rolls. Cover the top layer with the rest of the sauerkraut.

Pour the tomato juice over the top of the cabbage rolls and add enough water to just cover the rolls and sauerkraut.

Cook on a slow boil 1½ hours, adding water if needed.

SMOKED WILD PULLED PORK SHOULDER

An ongoing cooperative between the state and federal governments makes Kansas the only state with a wild-hog population either stable or in decline.

Meanwhile, these descendents of domestic swine are multiplying, and doing millions of dollars in damage, in about 40 other states. That means a lot of Kansas hunters often travel to places such as Oklahoma and Texas to hunt wild pigs.

If they treat it right, the meat they bring home can be good. I had it in a variety of Mexican dishes near the Rio Grande. Near the Everglades, my daughter and I had wild hog loin marinated in the juice of wild oranges.

My favorite way, though, is when my son smokes the shoulder of a large wild sow. The meat is a bit drier than domestic pork, but that means it's less fatty and greasy. I think it has more flavor.

WHAT YOU'LL NEED:

Prep time: 1 hour
Cooking time: 8-12 hours
Difficulty: Requires meat smoking skills,
specialized equipment

1 whole bone-in wild pork shoulder
5-9 lbs.

marinade injector

barbecue rub of choice

spray bottle

2-8 oz. apple *(or other flavored)* wood chunks

heavy-duty aluminum foil

2 cups chicken broth

1 cup pineapple juice

½ cup apple cider vinegar

Trim the pork shoulder to leave only fat, meat and bone. Mix the chicken broth, pineapple juice and vinegar. Inject into as many places as possible into the pork shoulder.

Pat the exterior dry with a paper towel and liberally season the entire shoulder with the rub. Cover in plastic wrap and place in the refrigerator until time to cook. Pour remaining injection liquid into a spray bottle for spritzing the meat later.

If possible, set the grill or smoker for indirect cooking and heat to 250 degrees. Add apple wood chunks. Place a pan of water under the pork shoulder, though beside the meat will work if needed.

Place the shoulder on the cooker's grill and try for a steady temperature of 225 degrees. After two hours, spritz the shoulder with the injection solution and repeat every 30 minutes. Make sure the water pan does not go dry.

Cook the shoulder until the meat is 190-200 degrees so it's the most tender. An inserted fork should twist 90 degrees easily.

A general timing rule is 1½ hours per pound at 225 degrees. If it's taking too long, when the meat is 140 to 150 degrees you can finish it in an oven set at 225 to 275 degrees.

Once the meat is at the desired temperature, wrap it in foil and let it rest 45 minutes. When ready, pull the meat off the bone, shredding over a pan to keep the juices with the meat. Sprinkle with some more rub, toss to mix and serve with barbecue sauce on the side.

PRONGHORN KABOBS

Pronghorn meat easily surpasses venison for quality when properly prepared afield. Every ounce of meat is to be cherished since pronghorn hunting permits are so difficult to get by lottery in Kansas, and because even a big pronghorn buck is only about as big as a small whitetail doe. Always grill pronghorn meat rather than use in an oven or crock pot.

The loins can be marinated and grilled like those of whitetail or mule deer. The roasts "kabob up" quite nicely.

Prairie castles – Gove County

WHAT YOU'LL NEED:

Prep time: 20-30 minutes, *plus marinating time*
Cooking time: 15-20 minutes
Difficulty: Requires moderate grilling skills

1 pronghorn roast
trimmed and cut into 2-inch cubes

1 ½ cups olive oil

⅔ cup low sodium soy sauce

¼ cup Worcestershire sauce

1 tsp. seasoned salt

1 tsp. black pepper

½ cup white wine

2 tbs. minced garlic

½ cup honey

1 large lime
juiced

1 each red, yellow and orange bell pepper
cut into chunks

1 large red onion
cut into chunks

wooden kabob skewers
soaked in water 1 hour

Pre-heat grill to medium-high, about 350 degrees.

Mix the oil, sauces, salt, pepper, wine, garlic, honey and lime juice in a sealable bag. Add the pronghorn meat, squeeze out the air and seal. Marinate in the refrigerator 6-10 hours.

Alternate as you slide pieces of meat and vegetables on the skewers. You'll probably have to double- or triple-up the vegetables to even out the amount of pronghorn.

Cook until the meat is medium-rare to medium, or 135 degrees, turning occasionally.

WILD PIG WITH CRANBERRY SAUCE

Faced with cooking the loin of an old boar, we turned to a simple marinade and one of my wife, Kathy's, favorite flavors.

WHAT YOU'LL NEED:

Prep time: 20 minutes
Cooking time: 20-25 minutes
Difficulty: Requires some grilling skills

wild pig loin
about 10 to 12 inches

1 cup cranberry juice

¼ cup soy sauce

½ cup wine *(or 7-Up)*

1 tsp. minced garlic

3-4 pieces of thin (low-sodium) bacon

toothpicks
soaked in water one hour

Mix the ingredients, pour into sealable bag, add meat, squeeze out air, and marinate 8-24 hours. The older the pig, the longer the better. Before grilling, make the following sauce.

1 tbs. butter

¼ cup onion
chopped

1 tbs. fresh rosemary
chopped

½ cup chicken broth

½ cup whole berry sauce

1 tbs. balsamic vinegar

Melt butter in skillet at medium-high. Add rosemary and onion until the onion softens. Add cranberry sauce, broth and vinegar. Whisk until the sauce melts. Low boil the sauce until it thickens enough to coat a spoon.

To cook the loin: Preheat grill to medium-high, about 350 degrees. Remove the loin from the marinade and wrap with bacon, securing with toothpicks. Grill to 150-degree core temperature on a digital meat thermometer, then remove.

Cut thin, and drizzle with sauce or serve sauce on the side.

WILD GAME SNACKS
VENISON JERKY

Most kinds of meat can be made into jerky or sausage. I don't delve much into such snacks because I simply value the roasts, steaks and burger of wild game too much. It's also possible to end up with a $300 processing bill if you go too far with commercially rendered snacks.

Still, every so often I'll whip up a batch of jerky in our food dehydrator.

I've done summer sausage, too, in our oven. Both are good ways to use up excess ground venison when a new season is approaching.

If you know you'll want to make some snack meat, have the processor grind some venison extra lean, as in half or less the beef or fat they normally include.

Autumn colors – Cross Timbers State Park

WHAT YOU'LL NEED:

Prep time: 30-60 minutes
Cooking time: 2-8 hours
Difficulty: Simple if you have a jerky gun
and dehydrator

5 lbs. lean venison

Hi Mountain Jerky Cure and Seasoning, original blend
(includes packets of seasoning and cure)

¼ cup liquid smoke

1 cup ice water

Jerky gun
with inch-wide nozzle

Heat dehydrator to 160 degrees.

In a large bowl, mix the venison with 1 cup ice water and liquid smoke. Mix in 4 tbs. jerky seasoning and 3 tbs. and 1 tsp. of jerky cure. Work the meat, seasoning and cure mixture well. Cover or wrap in plastic and leave in the refrigerator 8-24 hours.

The Hi Mountain package has directions for using an oven to cook the jerky if you don't have a food dehydrator.

Use the jerky gun to make long, flat lines of jerky on the shelves of the dehydrator.

Jerky should be done in about 8 hours. Bend a few sticks to check for doneness.

If the venison burger isn't lean, you may have to dab both sides of the jerky strips with paper towels a few times as they're cooking to absorb the fat.

NOTES:

► Works well with ground duck or goose. In fact, the original jerky shooter was invented by goose hunters around Emporia.

Z-BAR ONE BITES

I first tried this hurry-up recipe about 10 years ago when Keith Yearout, manager of the historic Z-Bar Ranch in Barber County, donated a wonderful buffalo roast to one of our wild-game dinners.

It's since been used on elk, moose, caribou, deer, goose, wild pig and

WHAT YOU'LL NEED:

Prep time: 10 minutes, *plus marinating time*
Cooking time: 15 minutes
Difficulty: Requires some grilling skills

2-3 lbs. wild game meat
trimmed as per directions, cut into 1-inch cubes

1 ripe fresh pineapple
cut into 1-inch cubes

1 bottle teriyaki marinade

thick, wooden kabob skewers
soaked in water 1 hour

After trimming away all of the fat and membrane, cut the wild game meat into 1-inch cubes. Do the same to the fresh pineapple once the skin and core have been removed.

Place the meat in a sealable bag with the marinade and let soak 1-3 hours.

Preheat grill to medium-high, about 350-400 degrees.

Alternate chunks of pineapple and meat, letting a cube of each touch the other but allowing a half-inch of space on the skewer between such combinations.

Cook on a well-seasoned grill turning every two minutes. Red meats, such as buffalo, elk and venison, will need to be cooked to medium-rare, though that may be as little as 5 minutes per side. You can slice into the edge of one cube to check.

The light meats, such as the wild pig and wild turkey, will need to be cooked to well done.

When the meat is done, use clean garden shears to snip the wooden skewers between pineapple/meat pairs.

Let stand a few minutes and serve on the sticks.

NOTES:

► One Bites make a great appetizer because people can hold one end of the cut skewer and remove the meat or pineapple with their mouth.

JALAPENO-AND-CHEESE SUMMER SAUSAGE

Jalapeno-and-cheese summer sausage and deer sticks have become popular. I'm a bit of a chili pepper wimp, but I've never had any such sausage that was too overpowering.

The family farm – Leavenworth County

WHAT YOU'LL NEED:

Prep time: 30 minutes, *plus extended wait*
Cooking time: 1 1/2 - 2 hours
Difficulty: Easy

3 lbs. lean ground venison

2 tsp. mustard seed

½ tsp. garlic powder

1 cup cold water

1 tsp. coarse ground pepper

1 tbs. liquid smoke

3 tbs. Morton's Tender Quick cure

1 cup shredded cheddar cheese

2 jalapenos
seeds removed, diced
(can add more or less for personal taste)

Mix water, mustard seed, garlic powder, pepper and liquid smoke in a large bowl. Next add venison, jalapenos and cheese until everything is blended together. It may take several minutes to be sure it's right.

Divide the mixture into three sections and roll into 2-inch logs. Wrap each log tightly in foil and refrigerate 1-2 days.

Pre-heat oven to 300 degrees.

When ready to cook, unwrap the logs and place them on a foil-lined baking sheet. Cook at 300 degrees about 1 1/2-2 hours, until the internal temperature is 160 degrees.

Remove and dab with paper towels if needed. Allow to come to room temperature before slicing. Can be vacuum-sealed and frozen with good results.

The return – Tallgrass Prairie National Reserve

WATERFOWL AND DOVES

Waterfowlers are the most hardy of those who mine enjoyment from the Kansas outdoors. We often arise when it's almost still yesterday, and drive three hours just to wade another hour through thick rushes to get deep in a swamp.

We work hard, battling knee-deep, boot-sucking mud or toting and placing more goose decoys than the population of some Kansas county seats.

And we do it in weather ranging from sweltering September days to January blizzards, when the temperature is 20 degrees below we-gotta-be-crazy.

Yet it seems a bargain to watch a string of mallards spiral down from the heavens and pack themselves in a hole we've broken in the ice.

Just as satisfactory is when Canada geese that look as big as small planes pass low enough that we feel the wind from their beating wings.

Those kinds of hunts are common in Kansas because of our great wetlands, an abundance of wheat, corn and other avian groceries, and an area that is a migrational main drag for millions of waterfowl.

But as revered as the birds are in the field, they're often resented in the kitchen. I get more complaints about "tough and gamey" ducks and geese than all other game combined. Yet done properly, they can be as flavorful as good beef and as tender as your heart the first time your new Lab puppy licks your face.

Snow geese – Quivira National Wildlife Refuge

Waterfowlers probably see more wildlife than any other kind of outdoors enthusiasts. We're out early, stay late, walk, wade or row the extra mile and just naturally hang in some of the wildest places in Kansas. Some of the wildest are in, and near, the Quivira National Wildlife Refuge.

This story was originally published on Nov. 17, 2007.

The Wichita Eagle

LYRICAL WILDLIFE

It's one of Mother Nature's finest choirs, and it's not easily forgotten. Before dawn, white-fronted geese begin their high staccato songs while sandhill cranes add monotone trilling. Canada geese add their traditional deep honks and snow geese their high-pitched yelps.

With the sun comes a crescendo heard for miles as they excitedly call louder and the roar of flushing wings joins the mix.

The half-million or more rising birds form living cyclones that reach far into the sky before heading to feed on fields beyond the horizon.

At the Quivira National Wildlife Refuge, so it usually goes in late November, when it rivals Yellowstone and the Alaskan tundra for wildlife viewing.

Since before the time of the Cheyenne and Pawnee, vast migrating flocks have stopped to rest and feed at the marshes, 70 miles as the sandhill crane flies northwest of Wichita.

Some recent falls and winters, nearly a million geese, cranes and ducks have stayed at the 22,000-acre refuge, along with pelicans, gulls and herons.

With the migrating birds come those that feed on them.

Snow-capped, mature bald eagles and their drab-brown juveniles can usually be seen around or over waterfowl, searching for birds too injured to fly.

And while the waterfowl and majestic eagles bring Quivira great fame, they're far from the only feathered wonders.

Near sunrise, acres of cattails spew clouds of blackbirds often hundreds of yards long, flying an avian ballet of dips and climbs and swirls on windy days.

Officially recognized as a "wetland of international importance" by biologists worldwide, Quivira's uplands also hold treasures.

More than 100 bird species, ranging from thumb-sized sparrows to waist-high wild turkeys, regularly call Quivira's prairies and woodlots home.

continued...

On sunny days, prairie dogs play peekaboo from burrows on the refuge's northeast corner.

Tracks in soft sand may show where shy bobcats, raccoons and coyotes pass.

A dawn or dusk visit about any time of year shows Quivira's healthy deer population.

A November trek, when the deer are breeding, may show old bucks that spend the rest of the year in hiding.

In hormone-induced stupors, 10-point and better bucks may stand so close to roads you can see strips of green bark in their antlers from duels with trees.

But remember Quivira's wildlife is truly wild, which means there are days when it's active and days when it seems to have disappeared.

The sight and scent of humans may push many animals from sight.

Fortunately they're very tolerant of enclosed observation blinds - especially those on wheels.

Slow drives through the uplands, eyes peeled for anything other than flaxen fall grass or vertical brush, could find deer, coyotes or more.

The eagles and waterfowl are best enjoyed by parking along the Wildlife Loop at Quivira's Big Salt Marsh.

Midday, with good binoculars, you'll probably see ducks swimming in huge rafts amid the marsh and crowds of sandhill cranes, geese and their accompanying eagles along the opposite shore.

But usually the first and last hour of a day, as they go and come in their great flocks from feeding, is the most enjoyable time to watch the show.

Be warned, though, if you lower the windows and quiet the car, the wild choir you hear could be the siren song that draws you to Quivira for many Novembers to come.

To most, it's truly that special.

Sunset sandhills – Quivira National Wildlife Refuge

1. Waterfowl meat is dark and course because the birds use their wings so much.

   Unlike domestic chicken or even wild pheasant, the dark meat means ducks, geese and doves should be treated and cooked more like beef.

2. Aging dark-meat birds a few days lets enzymes tenderize the meat, though few people have a way to ensure the meat stays a few degrees above freezing. Marinades are a simpler solution. Some mainly tenderize while others also impart an additional flavor. Both are used in following recipes.

3. Plucking takes time, but leaving the skin on the birds does help keep the birds moist in cooking. Plucked birds can be cut down the middle, removing the spine, for those who want to use them on the grill.

4. Cooking long, low and with plenty of moisture, such as in slow cookers, is a good option.

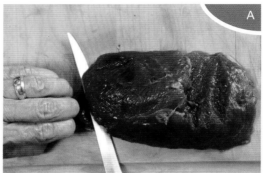

Trimming the membrane away from duck and goose fillets improves tenderness and flavor. Begin with the membrane side of the fillet and trim down.

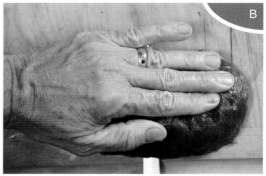

To keep the fillet whole, begin slicing about 1/16-inch above the bottom of the fillet, using your free hand to keep the meat level on the table. Slice across.

If fillets are to be cut into chunks, slice downward and over, near the bottom of the fillet.

It will become obvious how deeply you need to cut to remove the meat, leaving the membrane on the cutting board.

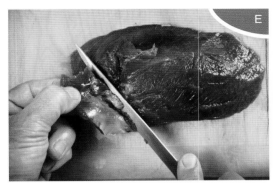

The gristly portion of a breast fillet that connects the meat to the wing is one of the toughest parts of the meat.

A V-shaped cut removes tough gristle from goose and duck.

For stuffing waterfowl breast fillets, lay fillets on their side, insert the knife and slice a deep pocket. Don't cut through the edges and leave the initial incision small.

For quicker grilling such as fajitas with large Canada geese, slice lengthwise through the fillets after the membrane is removed.

5. The fastest and easiest way to clean ducks is to separate the skin above the breastbone, pull the skin to each side and slice away the fillets. (I can clean a big mallard in about 45 seconds.) Keep in mind, though, that you can't legally fillet the meat from the ducks until you get home.

6. Clean red meat is good meat. Everything else should be trimmed away. Reasons for toughness include a sheet of membrane between the meat and the skin, and a chunk of gristle that joins the wing and breast. Both should be removed, especially in large ducks and geese.

7. When you go to high, dry heat with grilling, there is no middle ground. Cooked medium-rare to medium, migrant birds can be moist and well-flavored. The split second the temperature tips to medium-well or beyond, it will be dry, tough and taste like overcooked liver.

    For that reason, a good digital meat thermometer is as valuable to a waterfowler as insulated waders and fine spread of duck decoys. At around $20 to 50, the thermometer is much, much cheaper.

DUCK WITH PEACH SALSA

Fruit and waterfowl just seem to naturally go together, as is the case in this grilled-duck recipe.

Ice water – Neosho County

WHAT YOU'LL NEED: DUCK

Prep time: 20 minutes *plus marinating time*
Cooking time: 10-15 minutes
Difficulty: Requires some grilling skills

2 large or 4 smaller ducks, *trimmed as per instructions*

kosher salt

freshly ground pepper

powdered garlic

½ cup olive oil

4 tbs. freshly squeezed lime juice

1½ tsp. minced garlic

Season the ducks with salt and pepper well, and marginally with garlic. Rub in the seasonings. Place in a sealable bag, and add the olive oil and lime juice. Squeeze the air from the bag and let marinate 2-6 hours. While waiting, prepare the salsa.

WHAT YOU'LL NEED: SALSA

Prep time: 20 minutes
Cooking time: 5 minutes
Difficulty: Requires some grilling skills

3 fresh peaches, *halved, pits removed*

1 small mango, *halved, if available*

1 tbs. olive oil

1 tbs. freshly squeezed lime juice

1 tsp. honey

¼ cup red bell pepper

1 large poblano pepper, *seeded and minced*

⅓ cup red onion, *minced*

1 small ripe tomato, *diced*

1 tsp. minced garlic

⅓ cup fresh cilantro, *minced*

Heat grill to medium high. Rub 3 peach halves and 1 mango half in olive oil. Place open side down and grill about 5 minutes, until the fruit is lightly browned. Remove and cool.

Dice the grilled and ungrilled peach and mango halves. Place in plastic or glass container with remaining ingredients and 1 tbs. olive oil. Salt and pepper to taste. Let stand at room temperature before serving.

To cook the duck, remove from the marinade. Season again with salt and pepper. Grill a few minutes per side, turning as needed, until the meat is about 135 degrees.

Salsa can be served atop the ducks or on the side.

NOTES:

► 2 jalapenos can be used for those wanting more spice.

PEACE CREEK DUCK

A simple recipe that once had 80 of 81 non-duck lovers liking it. The lone exception admitted a bias. After that, we quit counting.

This a version of how writer Ron Spomer fixed prairie chickens about 25 years ago in Ashland, when chickens seemed as common in Clark County as meadowlarks. Three of us were stuck with no open cafe for lunch but six nice birds. Ron's version lacked the 7-Up and breading, but was one of the finest game meals I'd had to that point. I'd like to think some changes have made it even better.

Several times, I prepared this at The Hitchin' Post in Matfield Green as a freebie appetizer for friends. It got to where people recognized my pickup and stopped in, hoping to help themselves.

My favorite memory of serving the dish was after a cold day of hunting pheasants at Ringneck Ranch, near Tipton. I was doing a story on a group of Fort Riley soldiers just back from combat in the Middle East. They stood around the stove, grabbing Peace Creek samples like costumed kids reaching for Halloween candy. The huge batch of several mallards and pintails was gone before it reached the table.

We each gave personal thanks through prayer when the meal was served. Many grown men shed tears to hear how thankful some of the soldiers were to be with friends.

I was one of them.

WHAT YOU'LL NEED:

Prep time: 30 minutes
Cooking time: 20-30 minutes
Difficulty: Easy, *but you must monitor the duck*
so it doesn't get overcooked.

Breast meat from 2 big mallards,
or 4 medium-sized ducks or 8 teal,
trimmed as per directions, cut into 2-inch pieces

1 can 7-Up

1 large onion

1 large red bell pepper

1 large yellow bell pepper

1 handful white mushrooms

2 large jalapenos

1 tbs. bottled minced garlic

seasoned bread crumbs

olive oil

Put the duck pieces in a sealable bag, add 7-Up, squeeze out the air and seal tightly so the carbonation tenderizes the meat while the soft drink sweetens it. Marinade for 2-24 hours.

Clean, remove seeds from and cut the vegetables into quarter-sized pieces. Add ¼-inch of olive oil to a large skillet or wok, bring to medium-high heat and add the vegetables and garlic, stirring often. Remove the vegetables while there is just a bit of crispness remaining.

Add more oil if needed. Dredge the duck in the breadcrumbs, then add the duck meat to the hot oil, stirring often. After a few minutes remove a piece and cut to test of doneness. Remove duck from the heat while the meat is still pink inside and juicy. Mix in with cooked vegetables and serve.

NOTES:

► The recipe can be cooked with a stick of butter, half used for the vegetables and half for the meat, and no breading. Instead, use seasonings such as seasoned salt, garlic pepper or steak or cajun seasoning, sprinkled directly on the meat.

► Peace Creek Duck serves well as an appetizer, on a small plate with toothpicks.

► The recipe also works well with dove, greater prairie chicken or venison.

CEDAR CREST CANADA GOOSE

If Mike Hayden isn't the most avid sportsman in Kansas, he's certainly the most avid hunter and angler we've had as governor. He fished the ponds of Cedar Crest, the governor's mansion, and he was known to hustle back to the statehouse after an early-morning hunt for quail or ducks.

Hayden is a firm believer in using the game he gets. His favorite goose recipe is amazingly simple and danged good.

WHAT YOU'LL NEED:

Prep time: 20 minutes, *plus extended marinating time*
Cooking time: 15-30 minutes
Difficulty: Requires moderate grilling skills

4 Canada goose fillets
trimmed as per instructions

1 qt. buttermilk

½ small can condensed orange juice

1 tbs. of honey

1 tsp. of nutmeg

Marinate the goose in the buttermilk in a sealable bag 24-36 hours. The longer the better. Remove from the marinade and let the excess buttermilk drip off.

Heat grill to about 375 degrees. Grill, turning occasionally, until the meat is 135 degrees. Let sit a few minutes.

Thaw the ½ can of orange juice, and heat a partial amount in a small saucepan. Mix in the honey and nutmeg. Stir over heat until warm. Add more orange juice until you get your desired flavor.

It can either be drizzled over the goose or served as a dipping sauce.

Slice the goose meat about quarter-inch wide and serve.

GRILLED MESQUITE GOOSE WITH LIME AND VEGGIES INSIDE

Probably more eyebrows have been raised from this recipe than any I've shared. It works well with waterfowl, from mallard drakes on up to large Canada geese. It's my favorite way to cook small Canadas and white-fronted geese.

One of the main things is getting the fresh-squeezed lime juice flavoring and tenderizing the meat from the inside out. Also, as the meat grills, it pulls moisture and flavor from the veggies placed inside.

I first tried grilling goose this way with some white-fronted geese shot the last day of the season with Andy Fanter and Ed Markel, when clouds of migrating waterfowl were buzzing around one of Ed's Stafford County leases like bees around a shaken hive.

This is also a fantastic way to prepare sandhill crane, which is probably the most wary, yet best tasting, migratory bird

WHAT YOU'LL NEED:

Prep time: 30 minutes
Cooking time: 15-20 minutes
Difficulty: Requires some grilling skills

4-6 breast fillets small geese
or equivalent of mallards or big Canadas,
meat trimmed as per directions

1 lime *per bird*

1 bottle mesquite marinade

½ bottle liquid smoke

1 small onion

1 small red bell pepper

2 jalapeno peppers

½ tsp. minced garlic

1 package thinly-sliced (low sodium) bacon

toothpicks
soaked in water 1 hour

Make a 1½-inch horizontal incision with a sharp, pointed knife into the side of a flat fillet. Without widening the incision, make a sweeping motion with the end of the knife to cut a large pocket inside the fillet. Try not to cut through the edges of the meat except for the initial incision.

Stand fillet with incision up, and squeeze the juice of one quarter of a lime into the pocket. Carefully place in a sealable bag.

When all fillets have been so prepared, squeeze the remaining lime juice into the bag, squeeze out the air and let soak in the refrigerator for about 4-8 hours.

Next, add the mesquite marinade and liquid smoke and let soak another 4-8 hours.

Pre-heat seasoned grill to medium-high, about 350 degrees.

Puree vegetables and garlic in a food processor, or finely mince the veggies and mix in the garlic.

Carefully spoon the veggie mixture into the pockets cut into the fillets until the filling is about quarter-inch to half-inch deep when the fillet is flat. Wrap with the bacon and fasten with toothpicks.

Cooking time will vary based on the size of the fillets and amount of veggies inside, Often a total of 10-12 minutes will do.

Remove, let cool a few minutes. Slice thin with a sharp knife, and serve as medallions. The veggies should add as much color to the meal as they do flavor. Almost.

QUIVIRA GOOSE AND CABBAGE

Good hunting buddy Andy Fanter and I like to put this together in a crockpot in the evening, then plug it in when we leave for a hunt the next morning. It's a heck of a meal when our wives arrive home that evening.

Spring migration – Coffey County

WHAT YOU'LL NEED:

Prep time: 30 minutes
Cooking time: 8-12 hours
Difficulty: Easy

2 breast fillets, large Canada goose
trimmed as per directions

1 small head of cabbage
*stem system removed, top 5 or 6 leaves removed
and set aside. The rest is cut into 2-inch chunks*

1 onion
sliced into ¼-inch rings

1 red bell pepper
half sliced thin, the rest quartered

2 cups baby carrots

1 potato
quartered

1 can condensed French Onion soup

¼ tsp. minced garlic

meat tenderizer

salt

pepper

4 slices of bacon

toothpicks

After the meat is trimmed, slice a deep pocket in each fillet, coming in from the side. Sprinkle the inside of each pocket with tenderizer, salt and pepper. Split the minced garlic between the goose pockets, then fill the pockets with equal amounts sliced onion and red pepper.

Wrap each piece of meat with two pieces of bacon and fasten with toothpicks.

Lay three big cabbage leaves at the bottom of a slow cooker, and set the goose meat on top, pockets facing upwards. Pack remaining vegetables around the meat. Season all well with salt and pepper.

Pour the soup over everything, and add an extra ¼ can of water. Top with remaining cabbage. Cook on low 8-12 hours. Remove from slow cooker, remove the toothpicks and bacon, and slice thin.

NOTES:

► Potatoes can be omitted, and the meal may be served on a bed of mashed potatoes.

TEQUILA LIME GOOSE
IN CHIMICHURRI SAUCE

This recipe can be served as is, with the sauce on the side or add the grilled meat to serve as fajitas with thinly-sliced sweet peppers, jalapenos and onions on tortillas, with 1 tsp. chimichurri sauce per tortilla.

It would also work well as the meat, and bit of sauce, for a Mexican-style green salad.

WHAT YOU'LL NEED:

Prep time: 30 minutes, *plus extended marinating time*
Cooking time: 8-12 minutes
Difficulty: Requires some grilling skills

2 breast slabs from large Canada geese
trimmed per directions. Lay flat and slice in two horizontally to make 2 hand-sized pieces of meat about ½-inch thick

3 limes, *juiced*

½ cup gold tequila or 7-Up

2 jalapeños, *cleaned, minced*

3 tbs. extra virgin olive oil

½ tsp. kosher salt

½ tsp. ground pepper

½ tsp. minced garlic

FAJITAS

1 large onion

1 yellow bell pepper

1 red bell pepper

oil

tortillas

Cut the peppers and onion into thin slivers.

As the goose meat is finishing, pour a little oil into a skillet and sauté the peppers and onions until done. Heat the tortillas in a microwave or on the grill beside the goose.

CHIMICHURRI SAUCE

½ cup packed Italian parsley, *trimmed fine*

½ cup packed cilantro, *trimmed fine*

2 medium poblano chilies

1 tsp. minced garlic

2 tbs. red wine vinegar

½ cup extra virgin olive oil

1 tsp. kosher salt

½ tsp. black pepper

Place goose meat in a sealable bag and cover with all ingredients, well mixed, with air squeezed out. Place in refrigerator and marinate 4-12 hours. While that's marinating, prepare the sauce.

Place all of the sauce ingredients in a food processor and pulse until chopped and combined well. Refrigerate, removing about half-hour before eating so the sauce can warm to room temperature.

Pre-heat a well-seasoned grill at about 400 degrees, and cook the goose until medium-rare to medium (135-140 degrees). That may be only three minutes per side.

Let stand several minutes after removing, then slice into pieces about ¼-inch to ½-inch thick. Serve the chimichurri sauce on the side.

NOTES:

► Commercial Tequila Lime marinade is available, with no alcohol.

► 1 or 2 jalapenos may be substituted for the poblano chilies for those who like more spice.

EL CIELO SNOW GOOSE

One of the first goose recipes I was given, from my late friend Flip Phillips, is a good one. I've since had it served by several others at assorted wild game dinners, hunting cabins and get-togethers.

We've added a bit to suit our tastes. Base the amount of ingredients by how much snow goose you're preparing.

These can be great served as appetizers. Friends have cooked them while tailgating and gone through a bunch of birds in a hurry as the smell moves across the parking lot.

Migrants – Quivira National Wildlife Refuge

WHAT YOU'LL NEED:

Prep time: 30-45 minutes, *plus extended marinating time*
Cooking time: 10-20 minutes
Difficulty: Requires moderate grilling skills

snow goose breast fillets
trimmed as per directions, cut into finger-sized pieces

buttermilk

Worcestershire sauce

garlic powder

seasoned salt

jalapenos
cut in ¼-inch slivers (optional)

bacon
pieces cut in half

toothpicks
soaked in water 1 hour

After cutting into pieces, lay out the goose meat and liberally season with garlic powder and seasoned salt. Mix buttermilk and Worcestershire sauce until it's the color of hot cocoa, and make enough to completely cover the goose meat in a sealable bag.

Marinate 24-72 hours.

Heat grill to 350 degrees.

Wrap half-piece of bacon, with a sliver of jalapeno, around each piece of drained goose meat and fasten with a toothpick. Grill until medium-rare. It may only take a few minutes per side.

Serve with the toothpicks in. Best eaten with your fingers.

DOVE POPPERS

More than 30 years ago, on our way back from a great dove hunt near Baldwin City, hunting buddy Dick Hamilton shared the reason he was quick to take the birds if nobody wanted theirs.

"Wrap 'em in a piece of bacon and throw them on the grill. When the bacon's done, the dove is done. That's it," he said.

And that was it. I don't think anyone shared doves with Dick again after we tried his recipe.

WHAT YOU'LL NEED:

Prep time: 30 minutes, *plus extended marinating time*
Cooking time: 15-20 minutes
Difficulty: Requires some grilling skills

1 bottle mesquite marinade *(optional)*

10-15 doves
breasts filleted

1 package of bacon
pieces sliced in half

cream cheese

8-10 jalapenos
cut lengthwise seeds removed, about 3 inches long

steak seasoning

30 toothpicks
soaked in water 1 hour

Heat grill to about 350 degrees. Marinate dove fillets for 30 minutes, if desired. Remove and sprinkle with steak seasoning. Fill the inside of each jalapeno slice with cream cheese and lay a piece of dove atop it. Wrap in half piece of bacon, roll tight and fasten with a toothpick.

Put on the grill and remove when the dove meat is medium-rare to medium. Let sit a few minutes to cool. Remove the toothpick and eat.

NOTES:

► Can be done with sweet peppers and/or onion for those who don't want jalapenos.

► If dove meat is too rare, heat the popper in the microwave for a few seconds.

► Recipe also works well with teal or small pieces of venison.

SOY GOOSE (VENISON) JERKY

I once took a co-worker on a goose hunt, cleaned the geese and gave him the breasts from several big Canadas. A few days later, he handed me a stick of what I thought was beef jerky. It was from the geese.

We've since used a similar recipe on whitetail and mule deer venison with good results. The recipe has enough for one or two big geese, but it can be doubled or tripled.

WHAT YOU'LL NEED:

Prep time: 45 minutes, *plus extended marinating time*
Cooking time: 6-8 hours
Difficulty: Easy

4 goose fillets
trimmed as per directions and cut into ⅛-inch to ¼-inch slices

1 tsp. liquid smoke

1 tsp. seasoning salt

⅓ tsp. black pepper

1 tsp. meat tenderizer

1 tsp. onion powder

1 tsp. garlic powder

½ tsp. cayenne pepper
optional, can be adjusted for taste

¼ cup Worcestershire sauce

¼ cup soy sauce

Mix all the marinade ingredients in a sealable bag and add the goose strips. Marinate 12-24 hours. Place the slices in a dehydrator for 6-8 hours at 150-160 degrees.

For drying in an oven, place pans or foil at the bottom of the oven to catch any drippings. Run a toothpick through the end of each piece of jerky and hang from an oven rack. Cook at 150-170 degrees with the oven door cracked slightly. Check the meat every half-hour to make sure it doesn't get overcooked and dry. It may take 6 hours or so.

Let cool and place in sealable bags and store in the refrigerator.

Opening-day sunrise – Reno County

UPLAND GAME

Kansas is to an upland bird hunter what Disney World is to a small child. It can be a place where dreams come true, an experience unequalled.

We're home to some of the richest croplands in the world. But unlike most farm states, we still have millions of acres of wild grasslands and brush intermixed with all that milo, corn and wheat.

And amid that sometimes-perfect mixture of food and water, we have many thousands of rooster pheasants. With every flush, their brilliant colors and loud sounds take my breath even though I've experienced that rush so many times over more than 40 seasons.

As we are with pheasants and greater prairie chickens, Kansas is annually one of the three best bobwhite quail states. And a good quail trip is as classic a bird-hunting experience as created. Tight-sitting coveys of quail and pointing dogs go so well together that figuring which was better designed for the other is akin to the old chicken or the egg debate.

And we have plenty of upland game with fur as well as feather. A few decades ago, cottontails were the most popular game in America, but urban sprawl and clean farming has virtually wiped out most of the places they lived, what I call rabbitat, in most states.

But we still have enough rabbitat and rabbits that it's not uncommon to see an East Coast pickup, filled with beagles, on one of our public lands.

And where we have timber we have squirrels, and some of the best populations are on public lands. If you want solitude, be a Kansas squirrel hunter. Our season is nine months long and I once talked to a guy who hunted them weekly on public areas, and went three years before he encountered another hunter looking for bushy-tailed targets.

Blessedly, all of the mentioned birds, rabbits and squirrels are as easy to prepare as they can be delicious.

Hank's favorite duck – Neosho County

Bird dogs are one of the greatest joys of bird hunting, especially if it is your dog. As I've aged, I've noticed just how much I have in common with my aging Lab, Hank. This story was originally published on Jan. 27, 2013.

The Wichita Eagle

LESSONS FROM AN AGING HUNTING DOG

I often find the old dog lying near the fence, in a wallow he's hollowed through time. Ashen face on salt-and-pepper paws, Hank's again fallen asleep watching the street, waiting for me to come home.

I've always appreciated the deep loyalty only dogs can give. In Hank's case, it's a dedication I can't betray.

As long as he's willing to go, I won't be getting another retriever. I owe that to both of us after our thousands of hours afield.

Besides, we're not done with training. The ol' dog is still teaching me about living and aging.

At nearly 12, Hank's old for a big Lab. People have asked when the next pup is coming, so I'd have a hunting dog at its physical prime as Hank declined.

Hank was certainly something in his prime. Usually pushing 90 pounds, he once had a jaguar's build and athleticism.

Dense cattails parted like dust around him, he could make steady progress swimming against white caps and break ice with his front end.

Many times he was impressive vaulting a ditch or scaling a steep river bank, often with a big goose in his mouth.

He had brains to go with the brawn, thanks to off-season training sessions we both so loved.

Live or dead ducks could land within yards but he wouldn't budge until sent. Ignoring dead ducks floating near his face, with whistle

and hand signals, I often directed him to birds he hadn't seen fall 200 yards away.

Many times I stopped him mid-retrieve and had him lay down, sometimes neck-deep in cold water with a bird in his mouth, so he didn't spook a flock circling above. It got to where he'd do it on his own, having seen another flock before we did.

He seemed impervious to the cold, sometimes beside the blind caked in ice, except on a tail that wouldn't stop wagging.

For about nine years I considered such the norm, and judged hunts on limits filled and the quality of dog work.

But in the past two years Hank's flash has faded with his physique, hearing and endurance. Cold and heat crash his stamina, as do only a few retrieves.

Most of last season I watched the on-going decline with sadness and worried so much it detracted from our hunts.

But eventually I noticed Hank was as happy as ever. I realized for him, getting a chance to do what he loved to do, with those he loved, was more important than how well we did.

Like most Labs, Hank has moments of perpetual puppyhood, and the ability to find happiness in simplicity.

Days usually start with a happy dash across the driveway, seemingly convinced for the first time in about 4,000 mornings the newspaper will fly away if he doesn't hurry his fetch. A game of fetch the cap has him as proud as if carrying something with feathers.

This fall I noticed his tail snaps as hard after a birdless hunt as one with many limits. That made me realize I was headed in that direction myself.

Many of my adult autumns I traveled widely, heading to legendary places for glamorous fish and game.

continued...

Now I increasingly want to stick to Kansas, and game, places and friends I know well, including Hank.

But now our hunts are harder on both of us. To save Hank's comfort and our time, buddies often wade to get birds. We've added new hand signals since he can't hear the whistle well anymore.

I've lifted, tugged and pushed him more than any dog in about 45 years of serious hunting and training.

His sore muscles from once easy days often require medication. Yet this season there seems to be added anxiousness in the old dog. Many times I've heard him go from room to room until he finds me. When laying awake in the dark, I sometimes feel him checking on me.

He's always most at ease when we're heading afield. Sometimes it seems he realizes our time's limited.

I also wonder if dogs, like humans, face increased uncertainties as they age. Being around a loved one may ease some of the aches and pains, and knowledge that body is not what it used to be.

Twenty years ago I'm not sure I'd have realized that. But I do now, and I'm not adding to his uncertainty by bringing another puppy along.

Our trips are no longer non-stop hunting. I pace him on waterfowl retrieves and a half-hour in thick pheasant cover usually warrants a break.

But we've had some great moments.

Several times he's shown the wisdom of age can trump youthful enthusiasm with great retrieves, or close pheasant flushes after a long and diligent tracking job. That's good to know, because I'll never walk, shoot or call as well as I once did.

Some of our times are virtual trips down memory lane. Some places he obviously remembers because his tail pounds the pickup seat hard enough to raise dust when I stop the truck there.

I'm not sure what he remembers, but I know seeing and working those places triggers great memories for me.

As well as so many times with him, they've lead to smiles about a late friend, and of times long past when a son now grown and gone was a vital part of Hank's early hunts.

We've made it out scores of times this season, a fact I'll surely appreciate even more down the road. At Hank's age, hunting next season is just a hope. But far more important are current plans for a favored wetland for Sunday's close of duck season, and a few short trips to special places before pheasant and turkey seasons end Thursday. We won't be hunting hard, but we'll be out there.

As we go, I'll be cherishing great memories from the past, enjoying every aspect of our present, but not worrying about the future.

I think the old dog is training me pretty well.

UPDATE: Hank struggled through the 2013 summer, but rallied with the first cool mornings of September teal season. We picked our hunts and conditions, but had some great times afield that fall and winter.

He flushed and fetched a limit of four roosters near Newton the last day of pheasant season. His last retrieve may be on a big goose that sailed far and crashed, to fill an 11-year-old boy's limit that last day of that season.

The summer of 2014 has been hard on him. He's slipped a lot, and his end may be near. Or maybe a cool September morning at a marsh will rejuvenate him again.

Last-day limit – Harvey County

1. With little in the way of fat reserves, upland game is easier to dry out while cooking than domestic meats. Cooking low and long with moisture helps greatly.

2. Like most birds, pheasant and quail cook more easily if the meat is filleted off the bone. The legs and thighs of pheasants are excellent simmered down for soups and stock. Some people freeze them in a particular bag throughout the season, then use them when the season ends.

3. One of the biggest enemies of pheasant and quail meat are the jaws of an overzealous bird dog. A few chomps and what could have been a gourmet meal becomes pheasant burger. It's a problem I've never had in nearly 50 years of serious dog training and handling, but if you're afield with a bird masher, it may be time to carefully set the gun aside, and do your best to race the canine to the downed bird.

It's no fun to walk several miles for a rooster to flush within range, make a clean shot and have nothing to show for it on the dinner table.

PHEASANT MACAROONS

This idea came when Jacob Holem and his mom, Kimberly, served strips of turkey breast cooked in coconut oil. My wife, Kathy, loves coconut shrimp, so I did a little experimenting. She now says this is her favorite wild-game meal.

Of course, we both say that about something new several times a year.

WHAT YOU'LL NEED:

Prep time: 20 minutes
Cooking time: 30 minutes
Difficulty: Easy, *but can be messy*

2 pheasants, breast fillets
halved lengthwise

1 cup coconut milk, *plus 1 tbs. reserved*

½ tsp. minced garlic

1 tbs. lime juice

1 tbs. soy sauce

1 cup sweetened, shredded coconut flakes

1/2 cup panko bread crumbs

½ cup flour

½ tsp. salt

½ tsp. pepper

2 eggs
beaten

cooking spray

Soak pheasant in well-mixed combination of coconut milk, garlic, lime juice and soy sauce for 2-12 hours.

Preheat oven to 400 degrees. Lightly coat a baking dish with cooking spray. If possible, put the shredded coconut in a food processor and pulse into smaller pieces. Mix coconut with flour and panko bread crumbs. Beat eggs with the reserved coconut milk

Remove the meat from the coconut milk marinade, shaking off the excess. Dip in beaten egg, roll and press in shredded coconut mixture.

Place on sprayed baking dish and cook about 30 minutes. Remove and turn oven to broil.

Spray top of the pheasant with a light coating of cooking spray and place under broiler for a minute or two, or until the coconut gets crispy.

Serve with an Asian dipping sauce.

NOTES:

► Works well with similar-sized pieces of turkey breast meat, membrane removed.

LOIS' PHEASANT IN CREAM SAUCE

The Lois of this recipe is my beloved late mother-in-law, Lois Johnson, one of my dearest friends, biggest supporters and certainly the nicest person I ever met.

It's a recipe she used for decades, for birds shot by her husband, Bill, and son, Steve. I've improved it some, but it will always be her recipe.

Don't let the simpleness of the ingredients jade you against this recipe. Something magical happens when this combination of the two soups are blended and baked.

You will see and believe.

Snow bird – Harvey County

WHAT YOU'LL NEED:

Prep time: 30 minutes
Cooking time: 1 1/2 hours
Difficulty: Easy

2 pheasants, *breast and thighs filleted and cut into 2-inch to 3-inch pieces*

3 eggs
beaten

3 tbs. milk

2 cups flour
seasoned to preference

vegetable oil

2 cans cream of celery soup

1 can cream of mushroom soup

1½ soup cans of whole milk *or half-and-half*

one small onion

cooking spray

aluminum foil

one box long grain and wild rice mix

Heat skillet to medium-high (350 degrees).

Beat the eggs with the 3 tbs. of milk and place the meat in the mixture. Dredge in seasoned flour and cook in half-inch hot oil until browned crisp on each side. Drain on paper toweling.

Pre-heat oven to 350 degrees. Mix the soups and 1½ soup cans of whole milk or half-and-half. Blend completely.

Lightly spray the bottom of a baking dish (we used a 9-by-13 pan) with the cooking spray.

Arrange the browned pheasant in the bottom of the dish, and pour over the soup mixture. Thinly slice the onion and put atop the pheasant and liquid mixture.

Cover with foil. Bake for 1 1/2 hours. As the pheasant cooks, prepare the wild rice as per instructions. The meal is best served with the pheasant, and plenty of liquid, directly on a bed of wild rice to let the flavors mingle.

NOTES:

► Quail or wild turkey, cut into similar-sized pieces, work well with this recipe, as do chukar partridge.

LAZY J PHEASANT FINGERS

My first Wall Street Journal article,"Flush with Pheasants," was published in 1985.

Ray Sokolov, the Journal's Leisure & Arts editor, admitted seeing "Tonganoxie, KS" on the return address caught his attention amid the pile of proposals for articles.

Fortunately, Ray gave me a chance and my writing career a huge boost.

The article was about how families around Sublette were dealing with the farm crisis of the time by encouraging weeds to grow, leaving a few crops and guiding pheasant hunters.

The article was based out of Larry Leonard's Lazy J hunting service, the first of several successful shooting preserves in the Haskell County area.

Larry and David Holloway, his business partner, later became great friends and for several years I helped guide some large corporate groups. That allowed me to earn money working my dogs and meet people such as Nebraska coach Tom Osborne, golfer Tom Watson and football Hall of Famer Roger Staubach.

The guiding also provided scores of extra pheasants for our family dinner table. Probably more were cooked this way than any other because of the ease, speed and taste of the recipe.

The idea for the A1 sauce came from a baked fish recipe.

Double flush – Gove County

WHAT YOU'LL NEED:

Prep time: 15 minutes, *plus extended marinating time*
Cooking time: 20 minutes
Difficulty: Easy, *but a bit messy*

2 pheasants, *breast slabs and thighs filleted and cut into finger-sized pieces*

2 eggs

2 tbs. A1 Steak Sauce

2 tsp. milk

2 cups flour

salt

garlic pepper

cooking oil

ranch dressing

Soak in A1 and milk mixture 1-12 hours. As well as adding a unique flavor, the acidic nature of the steak sauce will tenderize the pheasant the longer it soaks.

Preheat a skillet, with about half-inch of cooking oil to medium-high (350-375 degrees).

Roll in flour seasoned with salt and garlic pepper. Fry until golden brown, then drain on paper towels. Serve with the ranch dressing as a dipping sauce.

NOTES:

► Works well with wild turkey breast meat, outer membrane removed, and cut into finger-sized pieces. Also for the breasts and whole thighs and legs of quail. For chukar partridge, a bird frequently released on shooting preserves, cut the meat like pheasant.

CLASSIC KANSAS QUAIL

For decades, I took Kansas wild quail hunting for granted. During college at the University of Kansas, we could head south of Lawrence and get eight birds a man easily. Just as successful were hunts around Abilene or Manhattan with Jon Hawkinson in the 1980s and early '90s.

Most of the quail were eaten the day they were shot. The flavor of those birds was never taken for granted.

But those days are gone because of habitat changes. Four or five quail is a special day now. No matter how many, I usually fix the birds the same way. Those few magical bites are even more cherished now than ever before.

Nice double – Stafford County

WHAT YOU'LL NEED:

Prep time: 20-30 minutes
Cooking time: 20 minutes
Difficulty: Easy

quail
breasts filleted and legs removed at the hip

buttermilk

flour

salt

pepper

garlic powder

vegetable oil

Soak the quail meat in the buttermilk 10-20 minutes. Dredge quail in flour seasoned with salt, pepper and garlic powder to taste.

Pour about ¼-inch to ½-inch of oil into a sturdy skillet and heat to medium-high. Add the pieces of quail. Turn when the bubbles around the bottom of the meat start to slow and the breading starts to turn crispy and brown. Remove when the other side is the same.

WILD SIDE LETTUCE WRAPS

The first thing that went through my mind when I had lettuce wraps at an Asian restaurant in Wichita was,"Wow, these are great." The second thing was,"I wonder what kind of wild game will work like this, too?"

The answer has been most kinds.

We'll go with pheasant because it's such a popular bird, but you could easily go with venison burger. Doves or teal would be good, too, stir-fried in a little seasoned olive oil or butter, removed while medium-rare and then diced.

Pride in his eyes – Scott County

WHAT YOU'LL NEED:

Prep time: 15-20 minutes
Cooking time: 1 hour
Difficulty: Easy

4 pheasant breast fillets
cut into ½-inch pieces

1 tsp. garlic powder

1 tsp. salt

1 tsp. black pepper

4 tbs. olive oil
equally divided

1 tsp. minced garlic

2 tbs. soy sauce

1 small onion
diced

¼ cup hoisin sauce

1 tbs. freshly grated ginger

1 tbs. rice wine vinegar

2 green onions
diced

½ cup cashew halves and pieces

Heat the olive oil to medium-high in the saucepan or skillet, add the pheasant and cook a few minutes, then stir in the all of the ingredients except the cashews. Cook until the onions are done, stirring well.

Add the remaining olive oil to a small skillet, heat to medium-high and add the cashews. Cook a few minutes until they're darker. Add to the meat mixture, combine well and cook until heated.

Serve with romaine or iceberg lettuce leaves, stems removed. Add the meat mixture to the center of the leaves, roll and eat.

STIR FRY
ON THE WILD SIDE

Many years ago, for her birthday, my wife, Kathy, wanted a Walkman so she could listen to music while exercising. I hadn't received a kitchen device I'd wanted for Christmas, so I bought it for her as a birthday gift.

So on her birthday, she unwrapped a sizable box and found that device. "What is this?" she half-asked, half-demanded.

"Can't you tell? "I responded. "It's a wok, man." I was about to cook myself out of trouble that evening.

Kathy has said it's been the best birthday present she's never used, referring to the hundreds of meals I've made.

I often use venison roasts or round steaks. It doesn't work as well with waterfowl. Commercial teriyaki marinade can make the cooking process much faster.

WHAT YOU'LL NEED:

Prep time: 20 minutes, *plus extended marinating time*
Cooking time: 20-30 minutes
Difficulty: Easy

1-1½ lbs. venison, pheasant, wild turkey breast

juice of one orange

½ cup low-sodium soy sauce

¼ cup honey

1 tbs. finely minced or grated fresh ginger

2 tbs. water

2 tsp. minced garlic

2 cups broccoli florets

1 medium onion

1 small yellow sweet pepper

1 cup sliced mushrooms

3 tbs. cooking oil

½ cup cashew pieces and halves

Trim wild game meat so it's free of unwanted membrane or fat, and marinate in a sealable bag with well-mixed portions of soy sauce, honey, fresh orange juice and ginger. Marinate 1-3 hours.

Heat wok or heavy skillet to medium-high, or 350 degrees.

Pour water into the bottom of a wok, or heavy skillet, add the vegetables and garlic and cook, stirring often until the vegetables are done, yet still a bit crunchy. Remove to a large bowl.

Wipe out the wok or skillet with a paper towel and add the cooking oil. Preheat to 375 degrees.

Remove the meat from the marinade, let the excess drip off for a few seconds and add to the wok or skillet. Cook, stirring often.

For red meat, such as venison, remove when still slightly pink in the center. That won't take long.

For pheasant and turkey, cook until the meat is done through, though slightly pink juices are OK. Add the meat to the bowl with the vegetables.

Add the last 1 tsp. of cooking oil to the wok or skillet and cook the cashews at about 375 degrees until they're well-browned and crisp. Add those to the bowl with the meat and vegetables and stir. Serve on a bed of rice.

NOTES:

► Customize the recipe for your favorite vegetables. I often add bok choy or cabbage.

KANSAS COTTONTAILS WITH WINE AND ROSEMARY

Cottontails are probably as tasty as anything that runs on the Kansas landscape or flies across our skies. The meat is light-colored and light-flavored, and as versatile in the kitchen as chicken.

Kansas hunters who like dog work but don't hunt rabbits are missing out. Working a brace of baying beagles is as enjoyable as following any pointer or retriever afield. The happy dogs work a rabbit's scent until it circles back to the hunter.

Some say they don't want to shoot cottontails because of the mess that occurs during cleaning. But the good parts can be cut off the carcass cleanly, without touching the insides, in a few minutes.

Simply skin the rabbit from the neck down. Slice the front legs away, pop the back legs out of socket and cut them away, too. With the rabbit on its belly, use a sharp knife to slice down each side of the spine, removing the loin the length of the rabbit.

Maybe if there's a fancy recipe, more people will take an interest in hunting rabbits in Kansas. Here you go.

The water hole - Pawnee County

WHAT YOU'LL NEED:

Prep time: 30-45 minutes, *plus marinating time*
Cooking time: 1 1/2 hours
Difficulty: Requires moderate grilling skills

2 cottontails
cut into described pieces

red wine vinegar

1 cup olive oil

2 tsp. minced garlic

1 tsp. salt

½ tsp. pepper

3-4 sprigs fresh rosemary

1 large lime
juiced

⅓ cup white wine

2 cups water

Place the rabbit pieces in a sealable bag. Pour in enough red wine vinegar to cover, remove the air, seal and marinate 90 minutes. Remove and pat dry.

Place the rabbit in a large skillet with hot oil until browned. Add the garlic and when it browns, pour in the wine.

Transfer it all, including the oil and garlic, to a pot with a tight-fitting lid and heat to a boil. Stir in the salt, pepper and rosemary. Slowly stir in the water. Cover tightly and simmer for 60-75 minutes. Add the lime juice.

When cooking is done, remove the pot from the heat and let the food sit about 10 minutes before serving.

CROCK POT BARBECUE COTTONTAIL

This recipe works on any kind of wild game, and we've enjoyed meals when it's been used on goose, duck, venison, squirrel, elk, deer and moose.

For cottontail preparation, skin the rabbits and take the meat off the back legs in chunks. Next, slice down each side of the spine and fillet off the loins. You can remove the front legs and simmer them in water at a low boil an hour or so to remove that meat, and add it, too.

The coffee is a natural tenderizer and won't impart any of its flavor into the meat.

Opening minutes – Scott County

WHAT YOU'LL NEED:

Prep time: 20 minutes
Cooking time: 6-8 hours
Difficulty: Easy

2 cottontails
meat cut from the bone

2 tbs. Worcestershire sauce

1 tbs. instant coffee

1 small onion
sliced into thin rings

2 tbs. liquid smoke

1 tsp. garlic powder

barbecue sauce

Place the chunks of rabbit meat in a crock pot. Add enough water to cover about half of the meat, then add the Worcestershire sauce, coffee, liquid smoke and garlic powder. Place the sliced onions atop the meat.

Cook 6-8 hours. Drain, shred the meat, place back in the crock pot and add enough barbecue sauce to thoroughly moisten. Reheat for 30 minutes to get warm.

It makes good sandwiches.

NOTES:

► On potentially tougher meat, such as goose or a venison roast, add another tablespoon of instant coffee and cook 8-10 hours before draining and shredding the meat. Be sure to remove the membrane from goose breast fillets. (That's covered in the chapter on cooking migrant game.)

► 1 cup of coffee can replace 1 tbs. of instant coffee granules.

BARBECUE LIMB CHICKEN

It was art time at a Manhattan preschool and kids were drawing their favorite foods. Some had drawn pizzas, some hamburgers or chicken nuggets. A teacher looked nervously as one little girl put the finishing touches on what was obviously a four-legged animal, covered in red.

"What is that?" the teacher asked, somewhat in horror.

"It's a squirrel," 4-year-old Lindsey Pearce replied.

"Is that blood all over it?" the teacher asked.

"No, silly, that's the barbecue sauce!" was Lindsey's quick response.

It's amazing how people look at meats differently. When I was a kid, fried squirrel was thought of as highly as fried quail, baked rabbit or a pheasant casserole. Deep in the Ozarks, in my grandmother's time, they were eaten often enough to be called "limb chicken."

Now, mention eating squirrel and people look at you like you've eaten their child's hamster. But I can promise you squirrels live a far cleaner lifestyle, and have a much cleaner diet, than most chickens.

Autumn oaks – Leavenworth County

WHAT YOU'LL NEED:

Prep time: 20 minutes
Cooking time: 4 hours
Difficulty: Requires basic grilling skills

2-3 squirrels
ribs removed, and cut up to pieces
of the back legs, front legs and the back

2 qts. flavored stock
can be chicken stock or leftover liquid
from cooking vegetables

olive oil

salt

pepper

barbecue sauce

Place the meat in a slow cooker and add the broth. Cook on low 3-4 hours until the meat starts to get tender. Remove the meat, dry it and rub lightly with olive oil.

Pre-heat grill to 350 degrees. Place the meat on the grill. Let cook a minute or two on each side and then baste with barbecue sauce and continue cooking.

The squirrel is done when the meat tears easily with a fork and the juices run clear.

NOTES:

► A pan of broth, on a low boil, can be used to tenderize the meat in about 1 hour.

► You can leave the meat longer in the broth. When it is tender enough to be easily pulled from the bones, it can be substituted for chicken in many recipes. Squirrel Helper or Limb Chicken Enchiladas, anyone?

► Despite Cousin Eddie's fears in "National Lampoon's Christmas Vacation," squirrel is NOT high in cholesterol.

Colors – Gray County

WILD TURKEY

It's an experience that must be heard to be believed, the effect of a wild turkey's gobble on the human body.

Chelsey Sherman obviously had gotten the experience one morning along Calvary Creek in Comanche County. She gasped for air, her eyes super-sized and body visibly trembling every time the tom gobbled at my calls.

At sunrise, the tom sailed the 200 yards to our hen decoy. On the ground, it gobbled loud enough to be felt as well as heard, and puffed into strut. Its tail was a plumed half-circle. Every body feather was raised and reflected more colors than a rooster pheasant.

It's because of such shows I've had hunters simply stop breathing, not be able to shoot or miss an easy shot by what seemed a zip code. Chelsey, thankfully, did her part.

Her father, Mark, hugged her hard and swung her around and around.

Clawing off her headnet, Chelsey tried to explain the experience, ending with,"...I thought I was going to die." Mark agreed it was exciting.

Chelsey grabbed him, looked at him hard and said, "Dad, you don't understand. My heart was pounding so hard I. Thought. I. Was. Going." A half-hour later, Chelsey was still shaking hard enough to send tremors through her orange juice at a cafe in Coldwater.

I've followed the Siren's Song of gobbling turkeys from Florida to California, and feel the most alive on a crisp spring morning when a tom is answering my calls.

From those travels, I've learned turkey hunting is about as good as it gets in Kansas, thanks to long seasons, liberal limits and many willing birds.

The meat of our birds can provide meals as high quality as the hunting experience.

Michael Pearce and Jacob Holem – Reno County

This article is about a friendship I developed with a boy who is as addicted to the outdoors as any kid I've seen in years. I put it in the wild turkey chapter because turkey hunting, spring and fall, have provided us some of our best memories.

This story was originally published on Feb. 9, 2014.

The Wichita Eagle

A FRIENDSHIP BORN ON THE OUTDOORS

Our friendship was born from his mother's desire for someone to take 11-year-old Jacob Holem hunting and fishing. The e-mail said the boy's dad died in 2006 and "all he's ever wanted is to be a hunter like his dad."

Five months later, Jake has used a crossbow to kill a rut-crazed trophy whitetail deer so close that we could see the wildness in its eyes. He filled all four of his fall turkey permits from excited flocks coming to calls. He has also shot ducks after watching them spiral down through a cottonwood canopy, to a rare open riffle on a mostly frozen river.

In more than 30 days afield, he's had "the best day of my life" seven times. The sixth-grader has also learned some life lessons not taught in classrooms.

Honestly, I've probably gotten more from our friendship than Jake.

AN EASY BOND TO BUILD

In early September, Kimberly Holem sent an e-mail to Mike Christensen, of Pass it On Outdoors Mentors, saying she'd failed at more than three years of trying to find an outdoors mentor for Jake. Christensen circulated her e-mail.

The timing was remarkable. Just the day before, I had decided to try to find a child to mentor through the seasons, trying to regain some of the joys of when my own kids were small.

Christensen put us in touch, and Kimberly said she'd do all she could to make schedules work, no matter the distance or time of day. She would make sure Jake was properly equipped.

"Some moms are soccer moms, but I'm an outdoors mom," she later said. "This is Jake's thing, all he wants to do. It's important to him so it's important to me."

Kimberly often thinks Jake has used all things outdoors as a connection to his dad. She wants to encourage that bond.

Jake and I bonded fast and easy.

At our first meeting to shoot targets, we learned we have much in common. I, too, lost a parent when I was young and understand what it's like to be an only child. We both were born with an instinctual love of the outdoors so strong it often overpowers our minds, but we both have struggled a lot to keep concentration in classrooms.

I wish we shared the same personality. Jake carries more innate happiness than most golden retrievers. Rare is the kid not smiling and positive, which are welcome traits after I've been on so many trips where others mostly complain.

It's also been refreshing to again see the outdoors through the eyes of a beginner who is thrilled just to get to go. We saw no deer on our first hunt, but as we left the blind Jake said,"That was fun," and asked if we could go again.

In these days when many hunts are measured by inches of antlers or limits, it was good to see someone get excited when a small buck with antlers the size of crawdad pinchers passed by.

I've bow-killed quality bucks the past three seasons, but none are as memorable as when that buck, the first Jake had seen while hunting, passed at 20 yards. The plan was for Jake to tap me twice if he saw a deer. Jake's dozen "taps" felt like a jackhammer. Buck fever hit the kid so hard, he actually had the cedar tree in which we were hiding shaking.

Two weeks later, Jake shot a buck larger than many hunters ever kill. But his reactions are more memorable than the buck's

continued...

size. Four times I hissed,"Shoot him," and four times, Jake hissed,"Now?" After so many years of dreaming of hunting, he couldn't believe what was happening.

After the shot, Jake's emotions exploded so hard he fell from his seat. His jabbing fingers kept missing the phone as he tried to text his mom the good news. I wasn't much better, and probably got more excited over Jake's buck than when I killed my biggest bull elk.

And after decades of sharing the fields with some who take hunting with life-and-death seriousness, I've enjoyed the silliness an 11-year-old can bring.

We've started a club he calls "Turkey Busters," complete with a song and dance. He's left turkey yelp messages on my phone to show his progress with a new call. Tuesday, we had a speakerphone calling lesson.

LIFE LESSONS AFIELD

Kimberly wanted Jake to learn hunting, not just go on guided hunts. That has meant many hours shooting targets, scouting, and placing blinds and stands. He has also learned to clean and cook his game. Like me, he's had to earn the privilege to access some special lands by working for the landowner.

Jake, often with his mom's help, has probably invested close to 40 hours on the property where he shot his buck and some turkeys. That includes working on food plots, filling feeders, gathering trash, clearing roads and running a line of trail cameras, then delivering the best photos to the landowner.

He's learning the best things in life are earned.

He knows his mom holds complete veto power over our trips if grades or home behavior slump.

His grades had his mother concerned, but are now good. A final grade of a B or better in math, the subject with which we've both struggled most, gets him a fly-fishing trip with me this summer.

We've had many conversations about how things he's encountered while hunting - such as making ethical decisions when no one is around, restraint, respect, and adhering to laws - will be important in many other areas through his life. Passing up shots that might be unsafe or just wound a bird is teaching him that doing nothing is often better than doing something wrong. Having held animals he's killed has shown him that some actions, once committed, can never be undone.

And he's learning the importance of setting goals, and working until they're a reality. If he builds enough strength by fall, he can use a compound for deer hunting. A long-term goal is to get strong enough to shoot a buck with his father's bow.

Jake has also made a pinky-swear pledge that he'll get good enough at calling to call in a turkey for his mom to shoot this spring, as partial repayment for her dedication to getting him outdoors.

Ongoing lessons are that his personality, strong work ethic and appreciation are solid ways to make friends. Every place we've been, Jake has been invited back. His thank-you notes and photos have opened more hunting and fishing opportunities.

I'm hoping in a few years, when he's more experienced, Jake enters a "pass it forward" stage and helps when I work with other beginners. A few decades after that, I have a feeling our roles will be reversed, and I'll be the one desperately wanting to go, but needing somebody to take me. I think Jake will do so.

Among so many other things, from our time afield, I think he's learning that really good friendships only strengthen through time.

UPDATE: Jake filled both of his spring turkey permits the first weekend of the season. Later he called in a bird I shot. He kept his promise, and called one in for his mom to shoot, too.

He ended the school year with an A in math, so we went fly fishing for trout in the Ozarks. As word of our friendship spread, more outdoors people came in to Jacob's life.

Strut – Butler County

1. Thankfully wild turkeys aren't the same as what you see at the grocery store. Their meat is free of additives, lean from living an active life and more flavorful. But since the birds have little fat, it is easy to dry out the breast meat. The legs, made of solid muscle, can be cooked to be as tough as a hammer.

   Or it can be all tender.

2. Wild turkeys smoke well, especially with water in the smoker and the skin left on the bird. But to me, plucking takes time away from when I could be fishing or looking for morel mushrooms.

3. If you're cleaning a spring bird afield, be sure to take a photo of your signed permit on the bird, and another of the entire, uncut animal to prove it was a legal bird, then register it online at *www.ksoutdoors.com*.

4. As with a pheasant, the skin can be sliced over the breastbone, pulled to the sides and the thick, white meat breast fillets removed. Leg and thighs can then be skinned, popped from the socket and cut away, too. The entire process takes less than five minutes.

5. The fillets will cook best if the membrane and gristle are removed, as with ducks and geese in the migrants chapter.

6. The white breast meat can be cut into smaller pieces and used in most chicken, pheasant or quail recipes. It's particularly good with the Lazy J Pheasant Fingers or Pheasant Macaroons recipes in the upland bird chapter. The legs and thighs simmer down to quality eating. Honest.

WILD TURKEY ROLLUPS

Listing all the ways I've prepared wild turkey breast would almost sound like Bubba explaining all the ways to fix shrimp to Forrest Gump.

Several of this book's pheasant recipes, including Lois' Pheasant in Cream Sauce, Lazy J Pheasant Fingers and Coconut Encrusted Pheasant, are great with wild turkey.

Another of our original recipes is to take long slices of breast meat, marinate them a bit, roll them on a thin strip of bacon and cook them on the grill. It can be done several ways as per the marinade.

Italian dressing: the easiest and original of our wild turkey roll ups.

Fajita style: mix three parts mesquite marinade with one part liquid smoke.

Asian style: mix three parts teriyaki marinade with pineapple juice.

Recently, my wife and I tried a raspberry marinade and side sauce combination that's unique and good.

WHAT YOU'LL NEED:

Prep time: 30-40 minutes, *plus extended marinating time*
Cooking time: 20-30 minutes
Difficulty: Requires some grilling skills

1 wild turkey breast fillet, *sliced into long, ½-inch strips with the membrane removed as per directions*

1 bottle raspberry vinaigrette salad dressing

8-10 strips thin (low sodium) bacon

short wooden kabob skewers
soaked in water 1 hour

Place the long breast strips in a sealable bag, pour in enough raspberry dressing to cover, squeeze out the air and seal. Marinate in refrigerator 4-12 hours. Just prior to grilling the meat, mix together this sauce.

SAUCE

¼ cup raspberry preserves

1 tbs. butter

2 tsp. red wine vinegar

1 tbs. ketchup

½ tsp. soy sauce

¼ tsp. prepared horseradish

½ tsp. minced garlic

1 cup fresh raspberries *(optional)*

Mix all of the ingredients, except the fresh raspberries, in a small sauce pan, using a whisk to completely stir in the preserves. Reserve the fresh raspberries. Heat until the butter is completely melted and all the ingredients are combined.

To cook the turkey, heat grill to 350 degrees.

Lay out a strip of bacon and lay a strip of turkey on top of it. Roll up together like a sleeping bag and fasten with a skewer. Two or three rollups can be placed per skewer.

Cook until juices no longer run pink from the rollups. Let cool a few minutes and serve with a bit of sauce spooned atop each rollup, adding a few fresh raspberries if desired.

ROCK CHALK GOBBLER GUMBO

Many people discard the legs and thighs of wild turkeys, thinking they're too tough to eat. Cooked long and low, they can be tender and one of the most flavorful of wild meats. This recipe is one of our favorite uses.

During his days at the University of Kansas, basketball All-American Wayne Simien repeatedly listed his mom's gumbo as his favorite food in media guides.

Since his mother, Margaret, was a friend long before her son was born, she gave me a tutorial in her own kitchen, a place she guards even better than her son did the basket at Allen Fieldhouse.

I've adapted it a bit, with her approval, to include plenty of wild game. This version usually makes 1½-2 gallons, though I often double it for special occasions. It never survives long in the newsroom on a cold, nasty day.

Turkey flush – Stafford County

WHAT YOU'LL NEED:

Prep time: 1 hour
Cooking time: 2-3 hours
Difficulty: Easy

legs and thighs from one wild turkey
separated at the joint

2 medium onions
cut into dime-sized pieces

2 celery stalks
cut into dime-sized pieces

Cajun or Creole seasoning

garlic powder

seasoned salt

½ wild turkey or 4 pheasant breast fillets
cut into bite-sized chunks

1½-2 lbs. smoked or Cajun-style sausage
cut into bite-sized chunks

2 heaping tbs. Savoie's Instant Roux

1-2 lbs. cooked shrimp
shells and tails removed

Place the turkey legs and thighs in a large stock pot or roaster oven, add the onion and celery and cover with water. Sprinkle the three spices until they cover the top of the water. Cover with a lid and cook at a low boil for 2-3 hours, checking every 30 minutes, until the turkey meat easily falls off the bones.

Add more water as needed.

Strain the contents, saving the liquid. When cool, remove the bones and tendons from the meat. Chop the meat into bite-sized pieces, then add the meat and vegetables back to the liquid.

Bring back to a simmer and add the turkey or pheasant breasts, and the sausage. Add enough water to cover the meat. Cook until the turkey or pheasant is tender.

In a separate pot or pan, bring a quart of water to a boil and stir in the instant roux. When it is completely dissolved, pour it into the gumbo and stir well.

Taste the broth. If it needs more "bite," add Cajun or Creole seasoning. If it needs more salt, add seasoned salt. Add the shrimp about 20 minutes before serving, stirred well.

Serve in a bowl of rice with cornbread on the side.

NOTES:

► The instant roux can be bought at www.cajungrocer.com or you can make your own.

► When doubling the recipe, rather than adding more legs and thighs I will add the other half of the wild turkey breast fillet and a small venison roast.

► One of the secrets to great gumbo is letting it season together, without the shrimp, a day or two. If it's cold enough, I'll just set the entire pan in our garage or on our deck.

► It freezes well in small plastic containers, which can be thawed then warmed in the microwave with a microwavable package of instant rice.

WILD TURKEY CRANBERRY SALAD

The flavors of roast turkey and cranberries have
probably gone together since the first Thanksgiving.
Here's a new twist that takes a lot less time and trouble
to fix. It's super healthy and pretty danged tasty, too.

WHAT YOU'LL NEED:

Prep time: 1 hour, *including making the salad, plus extended marinating time*

Cooking time: 1 1/2 hours

Difficulty: Easy

1 wild turkey breast fillet
trimmed as per directions

2 cups cranberry juice

1 cup white wine *(or 7-Up)*

½ cup olive oil

small oven cooking bag

dried rosemary

garlic pepper

A favorite green vegetable salad

1 bottle raspberry vinaigrette salad dressing

Mix the cranberry juice, olive oil and wine, and pour into a resealable plastic bag. Squeeze out the air and marinate in the refrigerator 8-24 hours.

Remove the turkey from the bag and let drip dry for a few seconds. Sprinkle with seasonings to taste.

Place in an oven bag as per bag instructions and bake at 350 degrees for 1½ hours.

When the meat is done, remove from the bag and let cool a few minutes. Slice into pinky-sized pieces and serve with your favorite blend of green salad, with sliced cherry tomatoes, feta cheese crumbles and croutons.

NOTES:

► Recipe could be used with 4 pheasant fillets, though cooking time can only be about 1 hour.

► Breast fillet could also be cut into three or four pieces and grilled.

First-turkey smile – Theresa Vail, Miss Kansas 2013
Chase County

FISH

Once known as part of the "Great American Desert," Kansas is a place of much water. Minnesota brags of being the "Land of 10,000 Lakes." Kansas has more than 100,000 impoundments.

Our waters range from skip-a-rock-across cow pasture ponds to reservoirs with up to 100 miles or more of shoreline. We are spider-webbed with flowing waters that range from tiny rivulets that flow down the major creases in our landscape to mighty rivers.

And the same nutrients that make our prairies and cropland some of the most productive in the nation make our fisheries some of most fertile waters for both quantity and quality.

Many of our lakes hold thick schools of crappie as big and thick as a $25 ribeye, except the fish have better flavor. At some reservoirs and rivers, anglers regularly use fry-worthy fish for bait to catch a catfish with a 5-gallon face.

Kansas fish are also accessible. Most of our 600-plus cities or towns offer a pond, lake or tiny stream where kids can thrill at the sight of watching a bobber bob, then disappear as it's pulled under by a bluegill or green sunfish. Most of us are just minutes away from where we can watch all heaven break loose when a bass or wiper explodes on a topwater lure, shattering the placid setting with a water-showering strike.

And for nearly every kind of fish caught, there are recipes that can make the eating as memorable, and enjoyable, as the catching – especially with a little basic knowledge.

Ms. Dorothy heads home. Wichita

I was wanting to write about someone who fished a lot of lakes in Wichita when I was introduced to Dorothy Jacobs. Within minutes of our first conversation I knew I'd found one of my favorite subjects.

Dorothy taught me several things about how to catch fish and offered many reminders about why catching fish isn't the most important part of fishing.

This story was originally published on July 7, 2008.

The Wichita Eagle

FISHING FOR THE SOUL:
Area lakes soothing for widow, cancer survivor

To nourish her body, Dorothy Jacobs fished as a child in southern Arkansas. To nourish her soul, she fishes as an adult in Wichita.

"When I'm on that water, I'm at peace," said Jacobs, 68. "It ain't the idea of me catching fish to eat."

The mother of 11 and grandmother of many – "It would take me quite awhile to count them all up," she explains – has had reasons to seek tranquillity.

The cancer survivor has broken her back and buried two husbands.

Nine family members have died within the past year, including a daughter and grandson.

She helps care for a chronically ill granddaughter.

"No question she's been through a lot," said her daughter, Janet Radig. "She's always been like that with fishing. It's like a job to her, but she really needs it. She has to go."

Going, Jacobs said, is when she feels her closest spiritual connection.

"I always do my best praying when I'm by that water," Jacobs said.

And she seeks such sanctuary often, seldom traveling far.

Jacobs frequents about all of Wichita's lakes regularly stocked by the Kansas Department of Wildlife, Parks and Tourism.

Her best catch, a flathead catfish of more than 20 pounds, came from one of those lakes.

She likes that Sedgwick County Park gives her easy access to several close waters.

On a recent morning, she pulled her rusted Oldsmobile into the parking lot of the lake on the north side of Chisholm Creek Park.

She'd spent much of the previous night caring for the granddaughter with sickle-cell anemia.

"She always wants to be with her grandma, and my grandbabies always come first," Jacobs said. "I got to take care of them."

Despite only a few hours of sleep, she was drawn to the water.

After all, she hadn't fished in about three days.

Into an old wheeled basket she placed a cushion for sitting, tackle box, water jug, cooler for fish and box of worms.

"I hate to think how many miles I've pulled this ol' cart," she said as she pulled it, some tires worn to bare wheels, down a mowed path. "I can go about anywhere I need to go with it."

That day, she went to a quiet cove apart from other anglers.

"I like to be by myself when I fish," she said. "When the fish

continued...

(are) biting, I don't have time to be talking, anyway."

Jacobs knows how to get them to bite. She has tiny hooks on the end of stout line.

"You don't need no big hook to catch big fish," she said. "It's all about how you handle that fish once he's on your line. You let that fish run, he'll wear himself out. He'll get tired before you do."

She baited the hooks with earthworms she had dug up, saying they catch more fish than store-bought nightcrawlers.

Jacobs pitched three bobbers and baited hooks a few yards from shore.

"I don't know why people think they should cast way out to the middle of the lake," she said. "Most of the fish are feeding by the shore."

And so they were.

It wasn't long before Jacobs detected signs of feeding fish.

"Just to see my line tighten up or that bobber moving, it's something I love to do," Jacobs said. "I don't see how people can't, but a lot sure don't."

Jacobs often predicted the species before she set the hook on a biting fish, saying each species had recognizable feeding patterns.

She caught about 20 fish, which included bluegill, channel catfish and bass.

She eats a lot of fish, and gives many to friends.

"I just call and tell them to come get their fish, I ain't cleaning them for them," she said. "I'll clean them for old people, and I give a lot to the elderly. A lot of them just don't have the strength in their hands anymore."

Jacobs chuckles at the thought that she's the same age as some of "the elderly."

"Going fishing's good for your body, I know it is," she said. "I've never had no high blood pressure, but everybody in my family, my brothers and sisters, have. I tell them being around water helps. They don't believe me."

They might if they watched her scamper up and down steep, eroded banks, or how easily she moves from spot to spot until she finds biting fish.

That she's fished nearly every mild-weather day for so many years surely helps.

"Old age doesn't mean you got to act old," she said. "I'm going to get all the joy I can out of my life. All I need is my poles and a lake."

UPDATE: Dorothy got joy out of her life for about another six years, dying on May 24, 2014. She'd been thrilled to have caught 60 fish the day before, according to her daughter, Janet Radig.

Checking her hook — Wichita

1. Some species of fish, such as crappie, bluegill and small to medium-sized walleye, are good to go as soon as the fillet leaves the fish. Others, not so much.

2. Severing the tail, just above the tail fin, to "bleed" any catfish makes the cleaning process much easier and ends the fish humanely.

3. Several species of fish, including white bass, striped bass, wipers and large catfish, have a dark line of flesh just below the skin. Removing that dark meat will remove most of the "fishy" taste from such species.

The dark meat can be left on the skin during filleting by angling the knife's blade up a bit as you cut across.

Be sure to keep the back of the blade flat against the skin, but angled slightly up as you cut along the bottom of the fillet.

The dark meat should be left on the skin (left). Any remaining dark meat can be trimmed from the fillet.

The dark meat on a fillet can make the meat strong and fishy tasting, but can be easily removed.

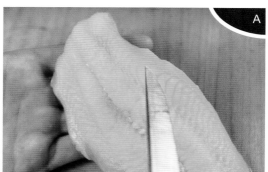

Catfish fillets often have a strip of yellow fat along the edges. It's the source of the fishy taste many people don't like.

While catfish usually have strong-tasting yellow fat, it's important to remove it from larger fish.

A few slices with a fillet knife easily slices away the yellow fat and improves the flavor

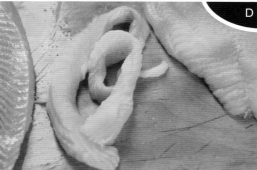

Be sure to discard the yellow fat. It makes good bait for other catfish.

4. All species of catfish, especially channel catfish, have edges of strong-tasting yellow fat that should be removed.

5. Care between the catch and cleaning of fish can impact the quality of the meat. Get them into a cooler with ice as soon as possible. Thoroughly chilled fish also clean easier than those at air temperature. If it's late, leaving them uncleaned on ice overnight works well.

6. Fish can get freezer burn quickly when unprotected, but can last quite awhile when frozen and submerged in water. Vacuum sealing preserves fish the longest.

REPUBLICAN RIVER GRILLED FISH TACOS

There must be something special about the water in the Republican River. Old-time accounts talk of flatheads the size of a buffalo calf, and hungry pioneers gorging themselves on channel cat caught on crude gear.

Now impounded as Milford Reservoir, those same waters are even better. The lake always has huge wipers that can make a big reel, and the angler holding it, scream like a scared child. The lake is Kansas' tops for blue catfish. Fish weighing 50 to 60 pounds seldom raise eyebrows. Friends assure me that 100-pound blues are there, growing larger every year.

Both blues and wipers have the firm, white meat perfect for fish tacos.

WHAT YOU'LL NEED:

Prep time: 30 minutes
Cooking time: 10-20 minutes
Difficulty: Requires moderate grilling skills

1-2 lb. of fish fillet
trimmed (see preparation tips)

2 limes
cut to be juiced and zested

½ tsp. minced garlic

¼ tsp. ground cumin

¼ tsp. chili powder

3 tbs. olive oil

kosher salt

ground black pepper

½ head of red cabbage
cored, and shredded or sliced extremely thin

½ medium red onion, sliced thin

⅓ cup chopped cilantro

1 cup diced ripe tomato

¼ cup chopped green onion

8 soft corn tortillas

guacamole

salsa

sour cream

Pre-heat a well-seasoned grill to medium-high (350 degrees).

Place fish in a sealable bag, then sprinkle with the zest and juice from one lime. Add the chili powder, cumin, garlic and 2 tbs. of the olive oil. Sprinkle with salt and pepper. Turn fish to make sure it's well-coated on both sides and place in the refrigerator 15 minutes to 1 hour.

Combine cabbage with onion, cilantro, chopped green onion and tomato. Sprinkle with zest and juice of a half lime. Drizzle with 1 tbs. olive oil, season with salt and pepper and toss lightly to combine.

Remove the fish from the marinade and place on the grill. (Foil boats can be used, with several small holes pierced in the bottom if worried about the fish sticking.)

Cook, without moving the fish, about three minutes per side. The underside should begin to turn white around the edges when it's time to turn the fish. Flip and cook the second side until the fish is white and flakes easily, with a temperature of 140 degrees. Move the fish to a warm plate and break up just before serving.

Cut remaining lime into wedges to be squeezed over the slaw and fish. Salsa, guacamole and sour cream can be added to suit individual tastes. Serve in folded warm tortillas or taco shells.

RITZY BAKED WIPER

No, it's not a fancy recipe from a luxurious Ritz-Carlton Hotel. It's a soooo-simple recipe from a striper fisherman near Lake Texoma nearly 30 years ago. The A1 adds just a bit of zesty flavor. The Ritz crackers provide a well-seasoned breading

WHAT YOU'LL NEED:

Prep time: 10 minutes
Cooking time: 10-12 minutes
Difficulty: Easy

1-2 lbs. wiper fillets
trimmed and cut into 4-inch pieces.

2-3 eggs

1-2 tbs. A1 steak sauce per egg

1 tube Ritz crackers

cooking spray

Whisk together the eggs and steak sauce. Let fish soak in the mixture 20 minutes to 2 hours.

Preheat oven to 350 degrees. Crush the crackers until well-powdered. Spray the bottom of a baking dish. Remove the fish from the liquid and shake off excess. Roll or push into cracker crumbs until coated well.

Place in sprayed baking dish and bake 10-12 minutes, checking to see if the fish flakes easily. When done (140 degrees), remove from heat and turn the oven on broil.

Spray a fine coating of cooking spray atop the fish and place a few inches below the broiler for a minute or two until crispy on top. Check it often.

NOTES:

► Works well with most fish fillets ¾-inch thick or thicker. Double the soaking time for largemouth bass and channel catfish.

GRILLED WALLEYE RIBEYES WITH LIME

No, fish don't come with things like steaks and roasts, but occasionally an angler lucks into a real pole bender of a fish that seems like it could.

That thick chunk of meat above Moby Walleye's rib cage doesn't need a lot of doctoring to be good. I like to cook them with this simple marinade so we get a good taste of the fish's true flavor.

WHAT YOU'LL NEED:

Prep time: 20 minutes
Cooking time: 10-15 minutes
Difficulty: Requires moderate grilling skills

1 thick, walleye or wiper "ribeye"
(portion above the ribs) per person
trimmed (see preparation tips)

½ cup extra virgin olive oil

2 large limes
cut to be juiced, zest removed

⅓ cup cilantro
chopped

¼ cup parsley
chopped

1 tsp. minced garlic

salt

black pepper

Pre-heat a well-seasoned grill to medium-high (350 degrees).

Combine the olive oil, lime zest and juice, garlic, cilantro and parsley in a sealable bag, with salt and pepper to taste. Add the fish to the marinade, turning to get well-coated. Squeeze out the air and let marinate 1-2 hours.

Grill on medium-high, turning when the bottom edge of the fillet begins to turn white. Remove when the internal temperature is 140-145 degrees and the fish flakes easily.

NOTES:

► Works well with big wipers, stripers, blue or flathead catfish

► The tag end of the fillet, from the ribs back, can be slivered and fried or cooked (see Ritzy Baked Wiper recipe).

CRAPPIE IN PECANS

There have been plenty of times I've gone nuts over crappie.
A few years ago, I started putting nuts on crappie fillets.
It works best with thick fillets, such as honest 1-pound
crappie or better.

(Note I said "honest," because crappie fishermen tend to give
their catches the big eye more than any other kind of angler.)

Black and white crappie – Glen Elder Reservoir

WHAT YOU'LL NEED:

Prep time: 10 minutes
Cooking time: 10-12 minutes
Difficulty: Easy

4 crappie fillets
each sliced in two pieces

¾ cup finely chopped pecans

3 tbs. butter
melted

cooking spray
butter flavored if possible

Preheat oven to 400 degrees. Soak fillets in cold water, rinse and pat dry. Coat the fillets well with melted butter. Press the fillets into chopped pecans until finely coated on all sides. Place in baking dish sprayed with butter-flavored cooking spray. Bake for 10-12 minutes.

NOTES:

► I've used this recipe with walleye, wiper and blue catfish fillets that have been trimmed. Cooking time may have to be adjusted depending on the thickness of the fillets.

WALLEYE WITH TOMATOES

Talk about good summer living: homegrown tomatoes and fresh walleye. Wow! This recipe came through a friend of a friend 25 years ago. Every few years I pull it out and wonder,"How could I possibly have forgotten about this?"

It's quick and healthy, but please don't hold that against it.

WHAT YOU'LL NEED:

Prep time: 15 minutes
Cooking time: 10 minutes
Difficulty: Easy

1½ lbs. walleye fillets
cut into 1-inch cubes

1 cup ripe, fresh tomatoes
chopped

1 cup olive oil

2 tbs. red wine vinegar

½ cup green onions
chopped

2 tbs. cilantro
chopped

½-1 tsp. minced garlic
(according to taste)

salt

black pepper

Combine 2 tbs. olive oil in a saucepan with onions, garlic, tomatoes, cilantro, vinegar, salt and pepper and saute on medium heat. Heat remaining oil in a frying pan over medium-high heat while seasoning the walleye with salt and pepper. Fry the walleye cubes for about one minute.

Quickly spoon the walleye cubes into the tomato/onion mixture and cook over medium heat until the walleye pieces are flaky and done.

Serve on rice or pasta.

NOTES:

► Works with any white, mild fish, including crappie and bluegill.

CATFISH IN CHIPS

This is a fast and easy way to bake catfish, or any other kind
of game fish, so it comes out crunchy and with a bit of spice.

Fishing at Elk River Falls – Elk County

WHAT YOU'LL NEED:

Prep time: 10 minutes
Cooking time: 10-12 minutes
Difficulty: Easy

1 lb. catfish, trimmed
(see preparation tips), cut into desired-sized pieces

2 cups jalapeno kettle-cooked potato chips
finely crushed

2 eggs

1 tbs. milk

cooking spray or spray butter

Pre-heat oven to 400 degrees. Dip the fish in the mixture of well-beaten milk and egg, then press into mixture of finely crushed potato chips until the fish is thoroughly covered. Place in a baking dish coated in cooking spray. Cook at 400 degrees until the fish flakes easily, usually about 12 minutes.

NOTES:

► Other flavors of potato chips can be used.

► Shredded cheese can also be sprinkled lightly in the crushed potato chips.

► Ranch salad dressing can be used in place of the egg/milk mixture.

MUSTARD FRIED CRAPPIE

I once told Eagle photo editor Brian Corn that someone still had crappie I had shared with them six months earlier.

Senior photographer Bo Rader looked up and said,"People can freeze crappie? When it gets to our house, it's lucky to make it to the refrigerator." His daughters wanted it cooked immediately.

Crappie is that good, and the time-honored way of dipped in a good breading is fantastic. Try running the fillets through a bath of yellow mustard to give it a bit more zest.

Our favorite commercial breading has been Andy's Fish Seasoning since Sherry Chisenhall, the Eagle's editor, shared some of what we call "magic dust" years ago.

I've attached a simple breading if needed.

Our lake – Leavenworth County

WHAT YOU'LL NEED:

Prep time: 10 minutes
Cooking time: 15 minutes
Difficulty: Easy

¼-½ lb. crappie fillets per person
cut into 5-inch pieces

1 cup yellow mustard

1 cup corn meal

1 cup flour

seasoned salt to taste

pepper to taste

vegetable oil

Mix the corn meal, flour, seasoned salt and pepper in a plastic bag. Coat each piece of crappie well with mustard, and then coat with breading.

Fry in about half-inch of oil at medium-high. Turn when fillets begin to get crisp, and remove when brown on both sides.

CAMP OUT TROUT

Most Kansas waters are too warm for trout to survive all year. Some are stocked to be caught in the fall and winter. Many Kansans travel to other states to catch the fish.

I caught my first on a scout trip to the Black Hills the week Neil Armstrong walked on the moon. This is how I ate the first trout, and many more that have followed. It's basically cooking the trout in a foil tent, which steams in the great ingredients..

I like to leave the head on the trout so I have an easy handle for removing the bones. No, I don't think it's looking at me because the eyes are there. It's dead, remember? Remove the head if you wish.

WHAT YOU'LL NEED:

Prep time: 20 minutes
Cooking time: 20 minutes
Difficulty: Easy

whole trout per person
entrails removed and thoroughly washed and cleaned

2 tbs. butter
melted

fresh dill weed

garlic pepper

lemon slices

¼ cup beer or white wine
(not used on the scout camp out – that came in college)

cooking spray

aluminum foil
in sections several inches longer than each trout

Pre-heat a grill to medium-high heat, about 350 degrees. Lay each trout atop the foil that's been lightly coated with cooking spray. Bring up the sides to create a foil tent. Brush the trout with the butter, sprinkle with garlic pepper and dill weed, including inside the rib cavity.

Squeeze 1 tbs. of fresh lemon juice over the fish, and cover fish with thin lemon slices. Add the beer or wine to the foil, and squeeze the foil so it's nearly touching on top.

Cook about 10-15 minutes.

When done, let cool a few minutes with the foil opened. Carefully peel the skin away with a fork. Then ease the meat away from the bones. When the entire skeleton is exposed, you should be able to gingerly lift the head and remove all of the bones from the fish.

NOTES:

► Foil tents can also be placed in hot coals at the edge of a campfire.

POOR MAN'S LOBSTER: CATFISH, STRIPER OR WIPER

OK, I was a bit skeptical the first time a friend in Oklahoma said we were going to eat striper and it would taste like lobster.

But it did, and the same simple recipe works on any fish with firm meat, such as catfish, striper or wipers. It really helps if the fillets are finger thick or better.

Should you ever luck into a bucket of mega-crustaceans, this is a great way to cook crawdads, too.

Make my day – Sand Creek, Harvey County

WHAT YOU'LL NEED:

Prep time: 20 minutes
Cooking time: 20 minutes
Difficulty: Easy

1-2 lbs. firm fillets
cut into bite-sized pieces

1 package crab/shrimp boil seasoning

2 tbs. sugar

¼ tsp. salt

sugar

1 stick butter
melted

1 lemon
cut into wedges.

Fix the boil per box instructions for spices and amount of water, then add the sugar and salt. Stir well. When the water is boiling well, gently place the catfish pieces into the water, such as lowering on a large spoon.

When the pieces float to the top, remove and sprinkle lightly with sugar. Serve to be dipped in melted butter and drizzled with a bit of lemon.

Cold day on warm water – Wolf Creek Nuclear Station

FROM THE EARTH

She was in her early 80s in the mid-1960s, but I can remember my great-grandmother walking around the farm yard picking "a mess o' greens" for dinner. Sometimes they were steamed like spinach and other times put into a salad.

Like a lot of her generation, Fannie Pearson (yes, that was her real name), knew there was a wealth of great, wild food to be picked growing from the Kansas soil. I remember her gathering lamb's quarters, dandelion leaves and wild onions for salads, among other things.

We also had pies made from family-picked wild blackberries and gooseberries. My dad and I often stopped and picked a handful of ripe mulberries or sweet wild strawberries heading to a fishing hole.

My friend and co-worker Beccy Tanner grew up eating lamb's quarters in Stafford County in the spring, and still picks it whenever she can.

As far as recipes or suggestions, I'm going to stick with the four plants I deal with the most.

Wild tomatillo – Douglas County

Wouldn't it be something if you've driven by the next big thing to bust cancer thousands of times on Kansas highways? Or if you're an outdoorsman or farmer, your life may someday be saved by a recognizable plant you see about every day afield?

It's still early in the process, but a plant common in Kansas holds great promise in the fight against cancer. The spring after I wrote this article, it started suddenly growing in my garden. I've let it be.

This story was originally published on Oct. 7, 2012.

The Wichita Eagle

MEDICINE FROM THE PRAIRIE

For decades the native prairie plant with tomato-like vines, and marbled-sized fruit covered in thin husks, has sprawled across the Kansas prairie in relative obscurity.

But scientists from around the world are now noticing the wild tomatillo, and wondering if it might provide a major medicinal breakthrough.

"We've found compounds from the wild tomatillo that have strong anti-cancer properties against breast cancer, skin cancer, thyroid cancer and brain cancer in our early studies," said Mark Cohen, cancer physician and research scientist who has been working with the plant for more than two years.

"It's very exciting because not only do those compounds occur naturally, but they're more potent than some drugs currently on the market for these diseases."

Cohen said initial research has been done against human cancer cells in laboratory containers and mice. Things are progressing well enough that human-based trials could begin in about two years, he said.

It seems the deeper the botanists, medicinal chemists and cancer researchers dig into wild tomatillos, the more promise the prairie plant holds.

"We've found 15 new molecules in the plant previously not known to science," said Barbara Timmermann, University of Kansas medicinal chemistry chair. "Nobody knew they existed and several of them are so active against cancer."

And it's not like this is some super-delicate plant from some far away corner of the Amazon.

Wild tomatillos, Physalis longifolia, are a tough, prolific prairie plant currently thriving over much of the central United States.

(They're related to a domestic variety of tomatillo, but scientists don't know if it has similar characteristics.)

But promised funding was abruptly cut less than halfway through the five-year research project.

"We are having fantastic data, and things are moving so well, then they just pulled the rug out from under us," Timmermann said, of money from Heartland Plant Innovations. "It's very unfortunate, and very disappointing."

NATURAL PHARMACY

The Native Medicinal Plant Research Program began in 2010 as a joint venture using the strengths of the Kansas Biological Survey, the KU School of Pharmacy and the KU School of Medicine.

Timmermann and Kelly Kindscher, a biological survey senior scientist, have long seen the Kansas prairies as a potential pharmacy waiting to be explored.

"Everybody has been going to the rain forest and other exotic places for research," said Timmermann, who has about 30 years of experience researching medicinal plants,"but we knew the Midwest had so many plants nobody had ever really looked at."

Kindscher, a noted expert on America's prairies, had also learned that for centuries native tribes were utilizing a number of plants for medicinal purposes before the state was settled.

"They weren't collecting them randomly," Kindscher said.

continued...

"They'd learned what to use, and used them in many cases fairly effectively."

He said modern research has shown most do indeed work.

Kindscher said any medicinal benefits found in plant compounds are mostly coincidental. Most are produced to protect the plant in some way or another.

"Plants can't run and they can't just grow spines if they don't have them, so they need some kind of chemical defense against being eaten by insects or something," he said.

They also may help them survive tough conditions, like floods and drought.

While Kindscher and crew eventually provided about 200 different species of prairie plants for testing, wild tomatillos quickly gained the most attention because of the findings in Timmermann's lab.

GREAT PROMISE

As well as testing how the wild tomatillo compounds perform against cancer, the plants were also tested to see how they react to other kinds of human cells.

It would be possible, Cohen said, for a compound to be very aggressive against cancer but too toxic to healthy human cells to become a viable treatment.

Fortunately, that hasn't been the case so far.

"It's very exciting that (wild tomatillo compounds) do have a strong potency effect against cancer and do not have significant toxicity against other cells so far in our evaluations," said Cohen, who is directing laboratory testing on the wild tomatillo compounds furnished by Timmermann.

Initially Cohen did so at the KU School of Medicine. He took the chores with him to a new job at the University of Michigan.

If all goes very well, Cohen said clinical trials with humans could begin within about two years. Wild tomatillo-based drugs could possibly hit the general market within about seven years.

It's too early to know how the medicine could be administered, if it passes all testing and trials.

Cohen said it could probably be injected into patients.

An oral wild tomatillo extract could be another option.

Kindscher said some of the highest levels of cancer-fighting compounds are found in the plant's fruit.

"The fruit is edible, and actually tastes very good," he said,"especially when it's ripe."

Acquiring enough of that fruit shouldn't be a problem in the future.

Wild tomatillos are so common Kindscher referred to them as "a common field weed" that grows on native prairies, pastures and farmlands, roughly from New Mexico to Montana and as far east as Ohio.

"It's probably one of the few (prairie) plants that are doing about as well as ever," he said. "It's common because it can grow in a lot of areas. Unlike a lot of prairie plants it does well on disturbed soils."

He said it grows well along roadsides or where the soil has been scarred by livestock.

It's common in farm fields, too. Kindscher is certain it could be grown commercially, too.

The perennial plant has proven to be hardy to temperature and rainfall extremes.

FUNDING CRUNCH

But one thing this miracle plant cannot do, is pay for its own research. All three scientists said funding is now their greatest worry.

Timmermann said Heartland Plant Innovations originally agreed to pay $5 million over five years to fund the research.

Heartland is a Manhattan-based bio-technology company backing plant-based research. In the spring, nearing the end of the program's second year, Timmermann was told funding would stop immediately.

"This just comes at a very bad time," she said. "This is when we should be growing." Currently the program is running on funding she'd saved from the previous two years.

Forrest Chumley, Heartland Plant Innovations' president, said the decision to stop the funding at about $2.5 million was a business decision.

"We're a for-profit company so we focus on projects where we can make the greatest difference. We've decided it's time to really focus on wheat development," he said. "We're really proud of what (the Native Medicinal Plant Research Program) has accomplished, and think it has great potential."

Chumley said budget cuts to the state-financed Kansas Bioscience Authority, one of his main sponsors, also left his group with less money.

Researchers are now searching for further funding.

"It's very exciting that this may represent some new cancer drugs," Cohen said. "Unfortunately our biggest challenge is now acquiring more funding so we can move things to the next level."

UPDATE: Kelly Kindscher, the main biologist in the story, reports wild tomatillo research is "slow-going, but still promising."

Is it the cure? – Douglas County

1. **PAW-PAWS**: They are found as far west as El Dorado, growing as thickets in moist areas deep in mature forests. They are easily recognizable by their foot-long dark green leaves. The 3- to 5-inch fruit usually ripens in the late summer to early fall, but raccoons often have the patches picked clean soon after ripening.

   They're great when cleaned, peeled and eaten raw, like the bananas they resemble. I've had them in puddings.

2. **PERSIMMONS:** The quarter-sized fruit reminds me of a fig in texture. They're sweet when ripe. Not ripe, not so much.
   Persimmon groves usually have clusters of 10- to 20-foot tall trees that grow on prairie hilltops as far west as Butler County, though they're most common in southeastern Kansas. The fruit stays attached so it's easy to see and shake loose persimmons well into fall.
   I normally put a few handfuls into a bag or can and snack on them like candy during a drive or a hunt. As a kid, I remember persimmon cookies and cakes at rural church gatherings.

3. **MORELS:** One of my favorite days in the Kansas outdoors was an April 1 when Jerrod, a KU student, called a gobbler out of Missouri and arrowed it after it strutted over the Kansas line at dawn. We then picked about 10 gallons of morels walking the ranch road.

   Morel mushrooms are found statewide, generally in areas with plenty of moisture and sunshine. Most good spots have a lot of leafy clutter flattened on the ground, and some decaying branches or trees. Other friends swear they find them around cedars.

   Never ask someone where they got their morels because they will lie. Do, though, make certain what you're picking is a true morel. That means it will be hollow through the stem and cap when cut lengthwise and the bottom of the cap is attached to the stem. The cap is covered in deep pits and ridges.

4. **SANDHILL PLUMS:** Spread by Mother Nature, Native Americans and pioneers, sandhill plums are scattered all across Kansas. Left to their own, they thrive best in, obviously, the rolling sandhills.

Depending on the geographic location and local variety, Kansas sandhill plums may ripen anytime from early July well into fall.

They often grow in fence lines and road ditches, but remember you must have the landowner's permission before picking plums. Most state parks and state wildlife areas have sandhill plum thickets open to public picking.

It's hard to confuse sandhill plums with other plants. If it's about chest-high and looks thicker than a jungle, it's probably what you're looking for.

5. There are plants and fruits in Kansas than can make you extremely ill, so do some research and make sure you can identify any fruit, berry or plant you're wanting to consume.

6. Remember that much of Kansas agricultural lands are sprayed with assorted fertilizers and herbicides. Don't eat anything that could have come in contact with such sprays.

SANDHILL PLUM JELLY

Sandhill plums are an ecosystem all to themselves. Their gnarly thickets are prime cover for myriad wildlife. In the winter, whitetail and mule deer bucks like to bed on the downwind side of a ridgetop plum thicket, where they can see trouble coming from their front and smell anything coming from their back.

For pheasants and quail, that same prickly canopy can be their only protection from avian threats when deep snow blankets the landscape.

During wet springs and summers, those same thickets bear a delicious, nickle-sized fruit that has delighted humans since the first natives wandered the prairies.

Keep in mind all wild plums picked are plums well-earned, as the branches holding the plums seem to pick back at your hands and arms, while chiggers and ticks feast on unsprayed legs.

I prefer to buy my sandhill plum jelly, the most famous product produced from the fruit. But it's not that difficult to make.

The Henderson House, a bed and breakfast in Stafford, has guided plum-picking trips for guests and helps them can their own jelly. This is the recipe furnished by Clare Moore, Henderson House owner. The recipe was his grandmother's.

WHAT YOU'LL NEED:

Prep time: 2-3 hours

Cooking time: 30 minutes to 1 hours
depending on equipment

Difficulty: Requires canning skills

6 cups sandhill plum juice,
produced with potato masher and system of strainers

8 cups white sugar

1 box dry pectin

Prepare a boiling water canner. Heat a small amount of water for the lids.

Heat the juice in a large stockpot. Stir in contents of one box of pectin and mix well. Bring to a rolling boil while stirring constantly.

Add sugar and stir until dissolved. Bring to a rolling boil, stirring constantly, and boil for exactly 1 minute. Remove from heat.

Ladle into jars. Wipe off rims and screw tops with a clean, damp cloth. Top each jar with a warm lid, then twist on a band until tight.

Process jars in a boiling water canner for 6 minutes. Let cool, undisturbed, on a wire rack or kitchen towel for 24 hours. Check jars for seal. Refrigerate any unsealed jars.

Label jars with contents and date. Store in a cool, dark place for up to 1 year. Refrigerate open jars and use within 3 weeks.

MAGNIFICENT MORELS

There are many outdoors memories that never leave your mind. One certainly is the first time you've sat down to a big platter of morel mushrooms. And from the time you leave that soon-emptied platter, you spend all of your time outdoors in the spring at least looking out of the corner of your eyes for more.

Depending on moisture and temperature patterns, some years it seems we have more morels than dandelions. Then we may go several springs with few.

In Kansas, I've picked them April 1 through mid-May, usually in moist woodlands, though I've found them in our yard, too.

There's no need to get fancy with the fixings. This same simple recipe has been successful for many generations.

WHAT YOU'LL NEED:

Prep time: 30 minutes, *mostly in cleaning*
Cooking time: 20 minutes
Difficulty: Easy

morel mushrooms,
tough part of the lower stem removed, cut in half lengthwise

1 stick of butter

finely ground saltine cracker crumbs

beaten eggs

splash of milk

Soak the morels in salt water overnight, then rinse gently in cold water and place on paper toweling to dry, outer side down.

Make the egg wash at a rate of one splash of milk per beaten egg and mix well. Soak the morels in the beaten egg and milk mixture. Melt the butter in a medium-high skillet. When the butter is melted, dredge the morels in the cracker crumbs and gently lay them in the butter. Turn when the bottom is golden brown and crisp. Turn the morel and repeat on the second side. Drain on paper towels before eating.

It takes fewer sandhill plums, but just as much care, for making what my friend of nearly 30 years, Spencer Tomb, calls Plum Bounce. There's a reason for the "bounce" part of the name.

It's an alcoholic drink best served in tiny amounts, like a sweet after-dinner drink. Taking a few sips became a fall ritual when we lived near Spencer in Manhattan.

WHAT YOU'LL NEED:

Prep time: 1 hour, *spread over several weeks*
Cooking time: None
Difficulty: Easy, *though takes daily maintenance*

EQUAL PARTS

sandhill plums
cleaned but whole

white sugar

vodka

Put the mixed ingredients in a glass jar, with the lid sealed well. The jar must be shaken every day for five weeks to dissolve the sugar. No need to put in the refrigerator. There's not a germ alive that could live in that mixture.

Prairie trail ride – Kanopolis State Park

My favorite rocks – Gove County

ACKNOWLEDGEMENTS

Wichita Eagle sports editor Kirk Seminoff was the primary editor for Michael Pearce's Taste of the Kansas Outdoors Cookbook. Sherry Chisenhall, the Eagle's editor and senior vice president/news, assisted in the editing and supervised the book project. John Boogert, the Eagle's former deputy editor, also helped with organization and supervision. All game meat was supplied by Michael Pearce. Kathy Pearce assisted with some of the cooking while finessing recipes. Jerrod Pearce smoked the meat for the pork shoulder recipe. Bo Rader contributed many hours of kitchen time to cook recipes for photography. Mikaela and Allie Rader helped with lighting and props for the food photography. Special thanks to Lyndsey Stafford of Armstrong Chamberlin for her work on the book design, and to Susan Armstrong and the team at Armstrong Chamberlin for their partnership in this project. Thank you to Shane Eustice, Warren Kreutziger and Mark Fowler, who provided fish for photography, and Lonny Travis, who provided morel mushrooms for photography. Thank you to Matt and Janelle Wiggers for sharing their property for outdoors photography.

ABOUT THE AUTHOR

Hoping to foster an interest in reading, a Tonganoxie, Kan., woman once bought her fishing-crazed, 6-year-old grandson a subscription to Outdoor Life magazine. It did that, and spawned Michael Pearce's career as Kansas' top outdoors writer.

Michael has been the outdoors writer and photographer for The Wichita Eagle since 2000. His Sunday Outdoors page in The Eagle, along with occasional front-page stories, bring the Kansas outdoors experience to Eagle readers. He also writes an outdoors blog on The Eagle's website, Kansas.com.

Michael, 56, is proud to say he's never had a "real" job. His articles on the outdoors began in college, when he was a contributor to Outdoor Life magazine. He later worked as a freelance journalist for the Wall Street Journal, which had him exploring some of the best hunting and fishing destinations around the world, as well as reporting on top conservation issues. He has also contributed to Sports Illustrated, Robb Report and many outdoors publications.

In his spare time, Michael does the same basic things he does for the newspaper – he hunts, he fishes, and he photographs wildlife. He jokes, "The only way I know if I'm working or playing is if I have to buy my own bait to go fishing."

Turning the fish and game he gets into fine meals, and teaching others how to do the same, is one of Michael's main passions. Many of his favorite recipes are in this cookbook.

His perfect day, he says, is to come home after a good trip afield and spend time with his wife, Kathy, and share a meal. The Pearces have lived in Newton, Kan., since 1993. Their grown children, Lindsey and Jerrod, share their father's passion for the outdoors.

INDEX